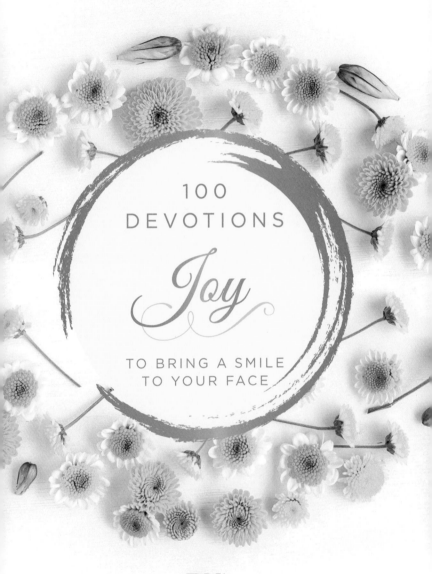

100 DEVOTIONS

Joy

TO BRING A SMILE TO YOUR FACE

PUBLISHING
NASHVILLE, TENNESSEE

Contents

Introduction

Joy is a funny little word. I don't mean that it's humorous but has a rather interesting definition that differs ever so slightly from one mind to the other depending upon one's perspective. For some, *joy* is a word used for those special occasions that capture the peak of one's happiness. For others, it might be that small flutter of positivity that builds in the moments of elation or excitement. Whatever the case may be, joy is not necessarily something that we feel impulsively. It is recognition. It is an intentional movement of one's heart to the noticing of the good in the bad, of the light in the darkness, of the joy in despair.

It is the celebration of one's health. It is recognizing the joy in one's work. It is the choosing to live on the bright side of a shadowy situation. Whether we'd like to admit it or not, joy is the outcome of strength in adversity, peace in uncertain times, courage in fearful situations, and love in spite of hate. That, in many ways, is what this book is all about.

Allow this devotional to be a reminder of the joy that comes from living a life that actively chooses joy. When struggles pop up in your life, take time to look at the situation, acknowledge the frustration, but instead of sitting in that frustrating moment, stand up, look to God, and choose joy!

Each devotional is accompanied with a message of looking at life's busyness and observing some of the obstacles that come with that busyness. Don't just allow the negativity of those situations to take root, but instead, discuss moving forward. We focus on the positivity of giving our frustrations to God. Simply put, we let go of our own understanding of a situation and place our faith in God. From this, we find joy. Joy is a product of ones faith. It is an outflow of putting one's trust in the Creator of the universe. It is an acknowledgment of the love that God shows each and every one of us every single day.

In many ways, joy is hidden from us. The anxiety and anger that fill our daily lives do their best to obscure our view from the joy of trusting in God. This devotional hopes to change that. It is not our intention to tell you everything is going to be all right with the world. This devotional was written with the hope and prayer that we would simply remind the reader that the world may seem like a tough competitor, but this battle is already over. It has already been one. Don't let the obstacles of the world overcome you. Don't allow the frustrations of this time fester and take root in your heart. Instead, trust God and know that in Him, you will find joy.

1

It's Too Hot for Creamer!

**The LORD is near the brokenhearted;
he saves those crushed in spirit.**

PSALM 34:18

Mary's father is close to eighty-five years old. He is a navy man and served in the military during some of the darkest times throughout modern history. Nevertheless, he is a navy man, and he's always eager to tell you about his experience serving his country. One way he does it is through basic storytelling. He is not a man of many stories, but he tells the ones he has with the same vigor of delivery as the first time it's told.

For him, it has always been about drinking coffee. He'll be quick to tell you that he doesn't want creamer in his coffee. He always says, "I worked in the engine room . . . too hot for creamer," and with a wink, "But it's never too hot for coffee." To be completely transparent, he's probably said that sentence once every other day, and yet, people still listen with respect and joy at simply hearing him speak about his life. You see, it was this year that Mary's father became a widower. His bride of nearly sixty years had gone home to be with the Lord, and Mary's father had started to decline mentally. It was something Mary would worry about daily. She would always wonder if he had taken his medicine or even if he had remembered to go to the cafeteria for a meal. Needless to say, when it came down to her father, she rarely spoke with a semblance of peace. Her voice always seemed to carry the slightest tremble when she would start to discuss her father.

A few years later, her father would join her mother. It would be something that would break her. She would feel alone and be tempted to have her grief develop into anger. Something, however, that would always stick out was dinnertime. After sharing a meal with her husband, they would share a small dessert and her husband would always request coffee. When she asked if he wanted coffee, he responded, "It's too hot for creamer, but never too hot for coffee!" She would laugh and, for the first time, realize the peace in knowing that her father was in the presence of the Almighty God that knows, full well, her father's coffee story, but is eager to hear it from a servant that has been good and faithful.

So many of us allow grief to come through the veil of worry. We do it so that when that grief hits, we feel that we've somehow prepared for it. Instead of allowing this grief to live in our hearts, replace it with joy in knowing that all that happens will one day work out for God's glory.

HELP ME TO BE ABLE TO HOLD ONTO THE MOMENTS OF JOY IN LIFE. HELP ME BE ABLE TO LOOK AT THE SEASONS YOU HAVE GIVEN ME AND ALLOW ME TO REMEMBER THE JOY OF THOSE SEASONS AND RESPOND IN GRATITUDE.

2

Report Cards

There is nothing better for a person than to eat, drink, and enjoy his work. I have seen that even this is from God's hand.

Ecclesiastes 2:24

For Kenny, report cards were a tumultuous time. He was a smart young man but would find difficulty in applying himself in certain classes: specifically science. Every nine weeks, he would greet the end of the quarter with apprehension and frustration. He would focus on the good of the report card but would always fear that his mother would only see the bad. He was not necessarily a troublemaker or a poor student. He still would come home with a few A's and a couple of B's, but science was always a low C or even a D. His last quarter, however, he made a decision. He would apply himself. He would study, and he would work to make sure that he earned the kind of grades that would separate him from the rest of the class.

For the next nine weeks, he would sit at the kitchen table as soon as he got home from school and study every day until dinner was served. He would open his textbook, take notes, and get ahead in classes that he would otherwise hate. On Saturdays, he would get up an hour earlier and spend an extra three hours rereading chapters that still gave him a few questions. From the outside looking in, he was a stellar student.

When the quarter was over, Kenny received the report card. In every class that was an A, the number climbed to a perfect score. In every class that was a B, he found it to be an A. He was overjoyed as his eyes went down the card. There were even a few notes attached that applauded his change in work ethic. His triumph, however, faded. His eyes drifted to the bottom of the card and he found his score in science. It was an 89. It was merely a B+, one point away from an A.

He went home to his mother, with his eyes pointed at the floor and gave her the card and continued on his way, dragging his feet, as he went to his room. After a few moments, he heard from the kitchen, "Kenny!" He expected the regular wrath that would come but instead found a table filled with treats that normally come with celebration.

He looked up to his mother with confusion, but she simply smiled and said, "I am so proud of the work you have done!" When he explained that he did not have perfect grades, she simply responded, "I was never looking for perfection. I only wanted your best." Kenny started to light up again and sat and enjoyed the celebration.

So many times, we feel that God wants us to be perfect. We feel that we constantly have to be the best in order for Him to even want us. This is just not the case. God only calls us to take up our crosses daily. Sure, we'll stumble. We will drift from the path, but if we are willing to get up each day, and pick up that cross, He is pleased with the effort.

HELP ME TO ACCEPT THAT I'M NOT PERFECT.
REMIND ME EACH DAY THAT YOU LOVE ME
NOT IN MY PERFECT DEVOTION TO YOU, BUT
IN MY EFFORT TO FOLLOW YOU EACH DAY.

3

Peanut Butter Dates

**Instead, I have calmed and quieted my
soul like a weaned child with its mother;
my soul is like a weaned child.**

Psalm 131:2

Tiffany has a nightly tradition after a long day at work. After she has gotten home, cooked a meal, and spent time with her husband, she has what she likes to call her "peanut butter date." It was once a time of "peanut butter meditation," but that would imply that she has the ability to spend that time alone. Her husband gives her as much alone time as she needs but something will still creep into her personal space.

Every night, like clockwork, she opens the cupboard, pulls out a jar of peanut butter, goes to the drawer and gets a spoon, and the moment she makes the iconic sound of twisting off the top of that jar, she always turns to find two giant brown eyes staring up at her. This little dog will wag his tail and sit patiently as his "fur mom" looks down at him with faux annoyance. Without fail, however, after eating her nightly spoonful of peanut butter, she always comes down to the kitchen floor, sits with her furry companion, and allows him to lick the spoon.

This is something that so many individuals would identify as an annoyance, but Tiffany would strongly disagree. For her, it is one of the few things that can bring her peace. For her, this little dog is simply a reminder of the times to be still and find gratitude for the blessings in her life. Sure, the job hours may crawl. Having to take care of every little thing may grow tedious, but she has come to enjoy the quiet that comes from simply sitting, and allowing her little buddy to come and lick the spoon.

So many times, we lose track of our ability to be able to simply be still. We live in a world where every little thing seems to be buzzing about us at all hours of the day. Frankly, it can be rather maddening. Something we must remember, though, is that we have a God that is as constant as a mountain. He is unmoving in His love for us. Honestly, I wonder what we look like to Him. Are we just buzzing by Him as He waits patiently for our love and time? Instead of trying to squeeze God into your life, think about taking a page from Tiffany. Have a seat, be quiet, and hear what He has for you.

LORD, GOD, ALLOW ME TO BE STILL. I KNOW
THERE ARE SO MANY THINGS IN MY LIFE THAT
I HAVE ALLOWED TO DISTRACT ME FROM
THE LOVE AND THE BLESSING YOU SHOW ME
DAILY. ALLOW ME TO BE QUIET AND LISTEN TO
WHAT YOU WOULD HAVE FOR ME. AMEN.

4

Seeking the Quiet

**"But when you pray, go into your private room, shut
your door, and pray to your Father who is in secret.
And your Father who sees in secret will reward you."**

MATTHEW 6:6

We live in a world where everything seems to be loud. Between working, handling all the family issues, and trying to take part in self-care, it almost seems like finding a time of quiet is an impossibility. For some of us, an escape is all that we can request. Some of us put that request in the form of vacations, or we escape certain volumes by distracting ourselves with others. The problem is, however, is that vacations are temporary and distractions keep us from addressing what needs to be handled. What we actually want is time.

We look for time to be able to be still. We seek out an extra minute here or there, just to be still. No matter what it is that we do, however, it seems this extra minute is one that always eludes us. For one mother, however, she seems to have found the secret. She has affectionately called it the family quiet time. It only lasts half an hour but has known to go over that time whenever quiet time morphs into nap time. It's a rather simple process. In her home, at four in the afternoon, she sets a timer on her phone. The rule is simple, you can do whatever you want, as long as it is quiet and doesn't involve video games, phones, or television. For her children, they will often use the time to pick up a book or work on homework. For her husband, he will go out into the garage and "tinker." For her, however, she sits in a guest room, in an armchair in the corner, and prays.

For the first few moments, she simply focuses on being quiet. Most of the time, coming to that quiet mind-set only takes a few moments, but occasionally, half of her time will be spent on just being still and letting go of all of the distractions that are floating around her mind. Whenever she gets to that stage, she then spends time thanking God for all of the blessings she can recall for that day. Then, toward the end, she dives into her Bible. She spends whatever time she has on her relationship with God. She started this little tradition a few years ago. There are, of course, a few days every now and again where she doesn't get to have that designated time and has to find it another way, but what's interesting is what that time has done. At first, it was very strict. It had to be thirty minutes, no more, no less. Then as the months came and went, the rigid time line started to become more fluid. Some days, the family would enjoy the quiet a little more than others. The thirty minutes might look more like an hour and a half. No matter what happened to the time line, though, the mother never changed the purpose of this time. She always spent it with God, giving her a peace beyond understanding.

FATHER, THANK YOU FOR THE QUIET
MOMENTS. REMIND ME TO USE THE QUIET
AS A TIME OF THANKFULNESS FOR ALL
THAT YOU DO IN MY LIFE. AMEN.

5

Summer Rides

**Do not be conformed to this age, but be transformed
by the renewing of your mind, so that you may discern
what is the good, pleasing, and perfect will of God.**

ROMANS 12:2

As Chelsea drove to her hometown, she admitted to herself that she was definitely dealing with some mixed emotions. In one regard, it was home, and there was no place like it. But in another sense, she had left for a reason. Cotton fields that would hold beauty to someone driving through only seemed to be reminiscent of the mundane life that she had left behind. She lived in the city now. There was no reason for her to actually be in this town, outside of family.

This week, however, was one of those reasons. Her grandmother would be turning ninety, and the family would gather to celebrate and use the time to reunite with those who had moved to other places.

Now, this town was the kind of place where supermarkets were social gatherings; town festivals occurred every season; and church was nonnegotiable. It was a town with three stoplights, a movie theater that could only sit just over a hundred people, and a mom-and-pop restaurant that only had five choices on the menu. For many visitors, this town would be seen as cozy, welcoming, and quaint. For Chelsea, it was awful.

She held on to this attitude even as she pulled into the driveway of her grandmother's home. It wouldn't be long until she saw family members pour out of the front door of the home and run to greet her as she stepped out of her car. As she was flooded with hugs, "Howdys," and kisses on cheeks, she would look up to the porch and see her father—sitting with her grandmother and smiling softly at his daughter.

It finally took her father saying, "Ya'll wanna go to the field?" for ears to be perked and grins to be formed. They all knew about "the field." It was some unused farmland that was about five miles out. They wouldn't do anything there as much as they would just enjoy the view. You see, in this field was a clearing that would allow viewers to watch the sun go down. It had become a summer tradition for her family to pile in truck beds and drive a few miles out to the field and watch those majestic sunsets.

For Chelsea, though, it was never about the field so much as it was about the ride. Though she acted a little put off by the idea, she got in the back of her father's truck, allowed the wind to carry her hair up and down, and after a few minutes on the road, her family would breathe a sigh of relief after hearing that trademark laugh that had seemed to have disappeared.

Like Chelsea, the longer and longer we find ourselves away from our heavenly Father, the easier it is for us to forget the joy that comes from our time with Him. Dive into your time with Him. Remember the moments that brought joy. You just might be surprised at what may come from it.

LORD, REMIND ME OF THE JOY THAT I DON'T EXPERIENCE OUT OF NEGLIGENCE OR EVEN SELFISHNESS. REMIND ME OF WHO YOU ARE, AND REMIND ME OF THE JOY I HAVE IN MY IDENTITY WITH YOU. AMEN.

6

Going Downhill

**You reveal the path of life to me; in
your presence is abundant joy; at your
right hand are eternal pleasures.**

PSALM 16:11

Just about every family has a tradition that is centered around the Thanksgiving season. For Connor, his family had the tradition of renting a large cabin in the woods for a few days and enjoying the Thanksgiving season there. Footballs were thrown. Hikes were taken, and bonfires were created. Connor loved Thanksgiving. He loved the reunion with family. He enjoyed the good meals, the games, and the conversations, but someone would always do something that would make their time "go downhill." It was a welcomed tradition in Connor's family.

This may sound like unpleasant news to most of us, but for Connor, it is his favorite part of the trip. "Going Downhill" is the activity of buying a sturdy laundry basket and sledding down hills that have been covered with orange and red leaves. The younger kids will pile into the basket until it inevitably breaks after colliding into a pile of leaves. The family can normally get ten to fifteen trips in before the basket is completely useless.

The tradition started when a wagon lost its wheel and all seemed lost in regards to an afternoon's entertainment. Connor's uncle, however, had a solution. He pulled a laundry basket out of the back of his car that he had used to transport games and snacks and put young Connor in the basket and shoved him down a hill. Connor's parents were furious until they heard the laughter coming from the basket that had now been engulfed in leaves. From there, a new tradition was born.

There's something about the kind of joy that can come from seemingly nowhere. It requires an attitude that is unwilling to allow circumstances to keep one from a sense of celebration. For many of us, we allow the world to sneak up on us and rob our joy. That is not how we are called to live. Like Connor's experience, there are going to be many moments where we "lose our wheel." How we respond to those moments determines whether or not we'll stay focused on the lost wheel or find joy in a new opportunity.

When it seems that life is taking you "downhill," what are some ways you can respond to find joy? Will you focus on the frustrations of a bad situation, or will you look around and find the joy that can come from a new opportunity?

LORD, ALLOW ME TO SEE THE GOOD IN THE BAD. ALLOW ME TO FIND JOY IN NEW OPPORTUNITIES, AND REMIND ME THAT MY VIEW OF A SITUATION IS ONLY AS BAD AS I DECIDE FOR IT TO BE.

7

Friendship Bracelets

**For we all stumble in many ways. If anyone
does not stumble in what he says, he is mature,
able also to control the whole body.**

JAMES 3:2

Do you know how to make friendship bracelets? It's pretty simple once you get the sequence down. Typically you take four separate strings and tie them together one after the other until it makes a pattern. The patterns can be as unique as the weaver wants them to be, but once a sequence has been set, it cannot change. That is probably the most difficult part of the process. It is not the weaving or the knot-tying so much as it is the actual moving forward with the sequence that has been decided from the beginning. It seems tedious, but there is a reward for those who have trusted the process to the very end. If every string has been placed in the chosen sequence, the bracelet will reveal a pattern that seems to have always existed.

What's interesting about these bracelets is always the creation of the first one. Someone with experience piques an interest in others by showing a nearly perfect design as an example and explains how to weave it. The sad reality of this is that the "first attempt" bracelet never looks anything like the perfection of a seasoned weaver. There are normally a few misplaced strings, or there are a couple of knots that were not tied with the same level of tightness as others. This does not normally keep people from trying again. There is never any blame put on the bracelet so much as it is put on the weaver's lack of trust in the process.

How many of us get frustrated with ourselves when our steps aren't perfect? We look at those who have been walking the same path with ease and assume they just have an easier time with it. Like the bracelets, there is not one of us who started walking the path of life and found the path easy, and yet, so many of us can think of someone that just seems to have it together. They read their Bible daily; they seem to have just enough time to give to others; or they simply have a way with their words when they pray publicly. It's easy for us to assume these people were just born good, but ask any one of them, and they will tell you the same: their first steps involved struggles, staggers, and stubs . . . just like yours.

The difference all comes down to the same thing: trust. For many of us, trusting in God is one of the most difficult things in the world because there is this knowledge that we will never be able to keep up to His standard. We will never be able to walk His path perfectly, and that's okay. Do you think these "perfect" people around you don't struggle? Do you think these people who have it all together don't trip and fall from time to time? They do! We all do! But there is a trust in the process. There is a trust in the path God has given them. Trust in Him. Find joy in knowing you are not the only one walking. As each step gets easier, as the weight seems to lighten, it is not *your* strength increasing. It is you inching nearer and nearer to God every day.

LORD, I KNOW I AM NOT PERFECT. I KNOW I AM FAR
FROM IT. I WANT TO BE CLOSER TO YOU. I WANT
TO WALK THE PATH YOU HAVE SET BEFORE ME.
GIVE ME THE STRENGTH TO DO SO, AND GIVE ME
THE DRIVE TO FOLLOW AFTER YOU DAILY. AMEN.

8

The Tablecloth

**He heals the brokenhearted and
bandages their wounds.**

PSALM 147:3

It's a little odd to talk about a funeral in a book about joy, and yet, here we are. Margaret's death was one that utterly shook the family. She was a light that helped brighten every family gathering. This is not to say that her family was hostile to one another. There was always a great deal of love between each of them, but nobody loved quite like Margaret. She left behind a husband, five children, seventeen grandchildren, and four great-grandchildren. Holidays were special times in her household, specifically because of comments that had come from a special tablecloth.

Margaret was not what you would call a seamstress. She was not one who would be considered a master with the needle and thread. This did not stop her from taking on the project of crafting together the tablecloth that had become part of the family experience. As her family grew, so did the line of tables that kept that family together at meals. With each growing family came a new table to help make the series of tables just a little bit longer to make just a little bit more room. Always the homemaker, Margaret started the creation of a large tablecloth to go over the mismatched tables to make everything just a little more uniform.

What's ironic about this statement is that the tablecloth was anything but uniform! As families grew, it was impossible to keep the pattern going the way it needed to be. So, she allowed the families to add on to it as they pleased. She would ask each grandchild when he or she was old enough to answer, "Which color would you want next?" With each answer, came a different color—constantly bringing a little more length to the cloth, and a little less rhythm to the pattern. This mismatched cloth had become a part of the family meal experience.

Weeks passed after Margaret's funeral until their first family gathering. There was an empty chair. Someone was missing for the first time instead of someone being added. For the family, it was a day of grief . . . not one of joy.

But then, Margaret's husband unrolled that tablecloth to cover all of the various tables and make one family. Tears began to fill their eyes, but before a solemn tone could fall upon the room, her husband said, "Margaret, I love you, but you were awful at sewing." Smirks formed, giggles erupted, and laughter bubbled over . . . and Margaret wouldn't have wanted it any other way. There are going to be seasons of loss in life. There are going to be moments where sadness seems natural, but in that moment, choose joy.

I AM STRUGGLING, GOD. ALLOW ME TO
LOOK PAST THE PAIN I AM CURRENTLY IN
AND GIVE ME THE ABILITY TO FIND JOY
IN THE DARKEST MOMENTS. AMEN.

9

Mom in High School

**"Do not remember the past events, pay
no attention to things of old."**

ISAIAH 43:18

Alison has always been a beautiful woman. Now in her fifties, she has achieved the honor of being known as the woman who "aged gracefully." From the people in this small town, Alison knows this is a backhanded compliment. From the perspective of her children, Alison has always been a woman who was poised, elegant, and sophisticated. She was not one who was afraid of getting in the dirt and doing the hard jobs, but she was always able to still stand with dignity and respect while carrying a triumphant smile to those who were ever in need of her assistance. Alison, however, was not always this way.

In an afternoon of reminiscing over photos of the past, Alison's daughters found a picture of a young woman and a young man. At first glance, they assumed it was someone else until they saw their father in the picture. Upon further examination, they would find that this stranger was, indeed, their mother! "Was this a Halloween party? Why was she wearing jeans with holes in them? What is with that hair? Have you ever seen her wear that much makeup? What about Dad? What is he wearing?" These were just some of the seemingly endless questions the girls had about their mother.

Alison couldn't help but burst into laughter. The girls nervously looked at each other as their normally poised mother was trying to regain her composure. After a few more moments of laughter, their mother finally returned to the woman that raised them. She looked at them and said, "Ladies, when you see something negative about your past, you can always laugh, knowing that this is not who you are anymore."

So many of us struggle with our past. Many of us probably thought of that moment as one of potential dread and are even thinking about certain photos that need to be destroyed. Don't! You are not your past! There are plenty of decisions each and every one of us has made that we regret, and there are decisions we are making now that we will definitely come to regret. The one thing we have to remember, though, is that we are not our decisions. We are not our mistakes!

We serve an incredible God who has seen past our awkward photos, has seen past our frustrating moments, has seen through our mistakes, and has chosen to love us in spite of ourselves. Let go of the identity that is held in your past and grab on to the identity that is placed in God.

LORD, I KNOW I AM NOT MY PAST. I KNOW YOU HAVE REDEEMED ME. REMIND ME TO TAKE HOLD OF YOU EACH AND EVERY DAY AND LEAVE THE PAST IN THE PAST. AMEN.

10

Study! Study!

**For am I now trying to persuade people, or God? Or
am I striving to please people? If I were still trying to
please people, I would not be a servant of Christ.**

GALATIANS 1:10

There are many culprits for the stress in our lives. For some, it may be family. For others, it could be a career, but ask any teenager, and they will probably come forward with an answer that points to a high-stakes test. Between SATs and ACTs and every letter in between, teens are thrown into the academic fires and feel as if they have to come out of the other end unscathed. No wonder most teenagers dread the classroom!

Mary Beth is no exception. Mary Beth is one of those who we all knew in school. She studies hard. She puts nearly all of her focus on her academic career. Extra-curricular activities are seen more as résumé builders instead of actual interests. Homework is mandatory. She is one of the only seniors in the building on "senior skip day." For Mary Beth, her work in high school will determine which college she attends. Her work in college will push her to certain internships. Her internships will garner the attention of potential employers, and these employers may help her in achieving her "dream job." Needless to say, Mary Beth's success as a student is paramount for her view of the future to succeed.

There is a little bit of a problem with this. She constantly worries. She never forgets, and she never lets go. She made a B on a spelling test in the fourth grade and she has yet to forgive the teacher. She also made a 99 on an essay that she still claims to have deserved a 100 during her freshman year. Mary Beth is a brilliant mind, but whenever she makes the slightest misstep, there is a focus on the error or on what could have been instead of the joy from the success that has already occurred.

This did not help with her preparation for her ACTs. Mary Beth had already taken it three times in an attempt to get a perfect score. This would be the last time she would be able to take it and put it on her application for college. The first time she made a 33, then a 34, and now a 35. One more should be just enough to get her to a perfect score of 36. A few weeks later after her fourth attempt, she would run to her mailbox, open an envelope, and scream at the sky as the number "35" mocked her effort. She had put so much effort into being perfect, and now it seemed that it was all for nothing.

Begrudgingly, she sent off her applications and received a letter back from the school of her choice a couple of months later. It was a thin envelope, so she expected the worst, but inside the envelope was a letter with a short message, "We don't look for perfect scores; we don't look for perfect people; we look for hard-workers. Relax. Enjoy your summer, and we'll see you in the fall."

How many times do we put so much effort in being perfect only to drive ourselves crazy with every instance of a shortcoming? No matter how hard we try, God loves us in spite of our shortcomings. So, yes, work hard; do your best; but know that you are loved . . . even when you fall.

LORD, ALLOW ME TO KNOW THAT I DON'T HAVE TO BE PERFECT FOR YOU. REMIND ME DAILY THAT YOU HAVE ALWAYS LOVED ME, EVEN IN THE MOMENTS WHEN I HAVE BEEN FAR FROM LOVABLE. AMEN.

11

Hiccups

**Rejoice always, pray constantly, give
thanks in everything; for this is God's
will for you in Christ Jesus.**

1 THESSALONIANS 5:16–18

We are all told that it could always be worse. That being said, I hate going to get my oil changed. It's never the oil change, of course. As so many of us know, there are many times that we take the car to our local mechanic or garage and find out there is always something else that needs our attention. No matter how careful we are as drivers, no matter how many potholes we avoid, no matter how many accidents we escape, there is always the never-ending reality that there is always something more to fix than what we initially expect.

The same can be said for Andrew when he brought in his car. Now, Andrew was a very financially responsible individual. He would buy a car with a couple thousand miles on it instead of one that was brand new. He lived in a neighborhood that may not have been the nicest, but was definitely afford-able. He would even shop around for parts and purchase them directly instead of just relying on the dealership to provide those parts. His plan for doing all of this was so he could, potentially, just outright buy his first home instead of taking out a loan. It was ambitious, but according to his plan, he would have enough to buy his first home in a matter of a few years.

Because of this careful lifestyle, he hated what he called "hiccups." Hiccups were these little unexpected financial setbacks that would cause him to alter his schedule slightly. It was never major, but it was always unwelcomed, and this day, a hiccup was coming.

As Andrew drove into the garage, he was only expecting an oil change and the replacement of a cabin filter. He was expecting to spend just over $150. While sitting in the waiting area, the mechanic approached him with a look of disappointment on his face. He said, "Your car is in great shape, but there's one problem." Obviously frustrated, Andrew asked what the problem was. The mechanic scratched his head and said, "I don't normally do this, but you should come to the garage and see for yourself."

Andrew panicked. What could it be? Was he going to have to rent a car for the night? How much was this going to cost him? He saw his car raised on a platform and dread filled his heart. The mechanic shined a light on his tire and showed a nail in one of the tires. What was remarkable is that the nail was less than a millimeter away from causing a blowout. The mechanic explained to him that a new tire would have cost him a little over $100, but since it had not done any serious damage, he could patch it for a little over $20. It was still a hiccup, but Andrew could manage . . . after all, it could've been a lot worse.

LORD, I ADMIT I HAVE BEEN GUILTY OF
LOOKING AT EVERY MISHAP AS A MAJOR ISSUE.
REMIND ME TO LOOK ON THE BRIGHT SIDE
AND SEEK OUT THE SILVER LINING TO ALL OF
THE FRUSTRATING SITUATIONS. AMEN.

12

The Drive-In

Rejoice in the Lord always. I will say it again: Rejoice!

PHILIPPIANS 4:4

In a small town in Middle Tennessee, there is a drive-in theater that attracts license plates from miles and miles away. It's the perfect location for an affordable outing. Couples use it for date nights. Families use it for family movies, and once a month, you can find a terrible horror movie from the 1950s. For Alex, it was the one place she loved the most. You see, her grandfather was the one who built this outdoor movie theater. When it was built, the majority of the farming town thought it was more than a little unrealistic. Her grandfather was mocked for using a perfectly good three-acre plot of land to be used, instead, as a "parking lot with two screens." Nevertheless, despite all of the town's ridicule, it would become the place to be every weekend.

Alex grew up sitting on a stool in the concession stand next to her grandparents every weekend. Her job was to say, "Enjoy the movie!" and she took that responsibility very seriously. As she grew older, her responsibilities would increase, but she would never forget to say, "Enjoy the movie!" For her, it was part of the experience. According to her grandfather, "Sometimes, people won't enjoy something unless they're reminded to . . ." This nugget of wisdom is something that she would carry into her adulthood.

It's been nearly twenty years since she said her first "Enjoy the movie!" Her grandparents have passed away and passed on leadership of the movie theater to Alex's parents. Alex has also passed on her first responsibility to her four-year-old son, who sits on a new stool, eagerly waiting to remind moviegoers to "Enjoy the movie." The movies are newer, the tickets are a little more expensive, and the snacks have changed from simply popcorn and candy to the ability to receive full meals, but one thing has always stayed the same. People still come from miles and miles to a field with a couple of screens and are greeted with smiles and a young child reminding each and every guest to "Enjoy the movie."

In life, even when we're going to events that should create joy, we often have to be reminded to actually enjoy the moment. There are going to be moments where that seems impossible, but God reminds us each and every day to choose joy. It may not always be easy, and sometimes, we may even need a bit of a nudge, but it doesn't change the fact that there are plenty of moments that will bring joy if we simply choose to accept them in the first place.

LORD, REMIND ME EACH AND EVERY DAY TO FIND JOY. GIVE ME MOMENTS WHERE THAT JOY IS OBVIOUS, AND IN THE MOMENTS THEY AREN'T, NUDGE ME IN THE DIRECTION OF A HEART THAT CHOOSES YOU AND THE JOY THAT KNOWING YOU BRINGS. AMEN.

13

The Discipline of Silence

**"Stop your fighting, and know that I am God,
exalted among the nations, exalted on the earth."**

PSALM 46:10

Many would assume that always having the right thing to say is a discipline worth having. That may be true, but sometimes, there is an even greater strength in recognizing the moments where no words are needed. Many of us often do our best to be able to give the right words but there is often a great joy that can come from a person simply giving no words and instead giving their time.

Many are not interested in being given advice in the middle of a stormy situation. We don't want to be preached at in the moments where frustration seems to reign. We've all heard our spouses say, "Sometimes, I just need you to listen." Silence is a virtue; it is the provider of one of the greatest joys in existence: understanding.

Think about the tone we use to describe these types of people. Do we speak of the loquacious with the same appreciation as the intentional listeners? If I were to say, "He always has something to say . . ." as opposed to "She is such a good listener . . .", which do you think garners more joy?

Though we may have an appreciation for both, there is something special about those who can give an ear, listen intently, and allow us to process our thoughts and emotions without interruption. There is always the temptation to jump in at every instance where we feel like the right word can be implemented, but it is often that the right word may not be ready to be received. That is what makes silence a joyous discipline. All of us can think of a moment where we were cut off midsentence only to be interrupted with well-meaning advice. It's infuriating! The joy, however, comes from the individual that makes us feel as if we've been heard.

God calls each and every one of us to share a good word. That is a given, but He also reminds us to treat one another with respect and dignity. To listen to someone without interruption is one of the most respectful things we can do for our loved ones who are in a time of distress. After all, we never hear from someone, "Thank you for just telling me what to do without allowing me to finish my thought." But we can almost always bet that there will be a thankful and joyous heart that comes from those who feel they've been respected and heard.

So, go out and listen. Before you give the perfect words that are filled with love and wisdom, make sure that you've practiced the discipline of silence and actually take the time to hear out your loved ones.

HOLY SPIRIT, REMIND ME EACH AND EVERY DAY THAT EVEN THOUGH YOU MAY HAVE GIVEN ME THE PERFECT WORDS TO SAY, I MAY NEED TO BE REMINDED OF THE PERFECT TIME TO SAY THEM. REMIND ME TO LISTEN BEFORE I SPEAK. REMIND ME TO ALLOW MY LOVED ONES TO FINISH THEIR THOUGHTS BEFORE I GIVE MINE. AMEN.

14

Bubble Party

**In every way I've shown you that it is necessary
to help the weak by laboring like this and to
remember the words of the Lord Jesus, because he
said, "It is more blessed to give than to receive."**

ACTS 20:35

As little Emma's seventh birthday approached, her father came to her and asked what she wanted for her birthday. He had some speculation on the matter. His daughter had been watching a certain movie just about every other night. He had inadvertently memorized the songs to the movie because of the constant repetition of the songs being played or sung by his little girl. He assumed it was going to be a toy that was tied to the movie in some form. The movie was popular with many children; so it was very apparent that this toy was going to be on the more expensive side. He did not make much at his current job, but that did not stop him from putting away a little bit here and there in the approaching months. Financially, he was prepared to make such a purchase.

The main character in the movie had the ability to make bubbles that could carry all of the characters all over the magical land that was the main setting of the movie. There was a specific bubble wand that could make large bubbles like the main character could. Even though it was a simple contraption, because it resembled the item in the movie, it was a little more on the expensive side. When her father asked what she wanted as they walked through the store, Emma walked right past the toy he had expected her to choose and chose a package of twenty regular bubble wands for a fraction of the price.

He was a little caught off guard by her decision, but when he asked her why she wouldn't choose the nicer version of the toy that she had chosen, she simply said, "Well, my friends are coming, and I want them to get a gift too." He couldn't be any more proud of his daughter than in that moment.

There is no question to the joy that can come from a generous heart. There is no need to know the rest of the story simply because we know that a spirit of generosity is one that is appreciated and loved no matter what is being given. People rarely care about an unexpected gift when they can tell that a gift is given out of generosity and not out of obligation. For little Emma, a bubble party was all she wanted. Not because she was interested in having spotlight or attention thrown on herself, but because she wanted to share her special day with others. Kids and parents could have attended and watched a little girl open a gift and enjoy her day. Instead, they would see a girl who was not interested in keeping joy for herself but was intentional on making sure that this joy would be shared.

LORD, REMIND ME TO ALWAYS BE GENEROUS.
EVEN WHEN THE MOMENTS OF JOY MIGHT BE
SPECIFICALLY FOR ME, ALLOW ME TO CONSTANTLY
SHARE THAT JOY WITH OTHERS. AMEN.

15

That Guy

**"Follow the whole instruction the LORD your God
has commanded you, so that you may live, prosper,
and have a long life in the land you will possess."**

DEUTERONOMY 5:33

Jordan will admit to you that he was out of shape. He was not in any kind
of condition to take on twenty-six yards, let alone twenty-six miles. He had
always talked about wanting to get in shape. He had always intended to lose
the weight, but training for a marathon seemed a bit extreme. He was not that
kind of guy. He was not the running type. He was not the athletic type. He
just wasn't *that* guy. And yet, here he was, ten months before the race, on a
treadmill, sweating, wheezing, and grunting his way to a half-mile. It was awful,
and he believed he would regret every second of it.

Each day, he moved up a tenth of a mile in distance. His first day was a
half-mile; the next day was six tenths of a mile. The next was seven tenths and
so forth. After a month, he was able to run a 5K. There was still a little bit of
heavy breathing and he did not have the quickest time, but nevertheless, he
saw signs of progress.

At the end of three months, he had conquered ten miles. He noticed
that he was a little quicker with each mile and didn't really start having signs of
fatigue until he was on his seventh mile.

At the end of seven months, he ran his first marathon outside of a race. He had another three months to prepare for the race, and here he was running the distance of the race on his own.

During his last two months, his focus began to shift to speed. He had moved from the attitude of simply finishing the race to wanting to be a competitor. He started learning how to use the terrain of the race to his advantage. Hills offered a little bit of resistance but offered a great deal of speed on the other side. Signs became checkpoints for testing the strength of one's speed. Jordan, as much as his past self would hate to admit it, had become *that* guy . . . and he couldn't be happier.

As Christians, so many of us are afraid of being *that* believer. We don't want to come across as a fanatic, and because of that, we almost instinctively hide our light from the world. The fact is, we are all called to shine. We are all called to be a light into a dark world. So, out of some false respect for the world, we don't read our Bible in public; our prayers at meals are quick and impersonal; and heaven forbid we discuss our faith openly. Like Jordan's avoidance of training for a race, we don't realize the joy that comes from living out our faith. Just as Jordan discovered his new life and joy in running the race, allow yourself to discover the joy of openly walking with God.

LORD, SHOW ME THE JOY THAT COMES FROM KNOWING YOU AND FOLLOWING YOU OPENLY. LET THE LIGHT YOU HAVE GIVEN ME SHINE BRIGHTLY TO OTHERS AND ALLOW ME TO FIND THE JOY IN GETTING CLOSER AND CLOSER TO YOU.

16

Stargazing

Our God is in heaven and does whatever he pleases.

PSALM 115:3

In Sedona, Arizona, you can find a campground that claims to be the darkest place in the United States. This can be a little disconcerting for some, but for many campers, it is one of the necessary wonders that all outdoorsmen need to experience. During the day, it's just a desert. There's a large amount of dirt, quite a few cacti, quite a few awe-inspiring rock formations, and one big open sky. At night, however, the dirt cools, the cacti fade in with the background, the formations turn into silhouettes, and this big open sky removes the sun and is instead lit up with countless stars that are normally hidden with light pollution.

For nonbelievers who visit the area, it is an overwhelming picture of an ever-expanding cosmos that will never be understood. Each star represents a system that has yet to be discovered. Each visible track of the Milky Way only reminds the viewer that we are only one infinitesimal part of a number of countless galaxies. These galaxies are moving between even more countless starts that are heating undiscovered planets in a universe that will never be mapped completely. To the Christian, it is only one of countless creations that God has placed in existence.

This could seem overwhelming to many people that look up at the stars and wonder, but for Christians, the only overwhelming emotion to feel is one of love. When we know there is a God who has created every grain of dirt, every plant, every rock formation, and every star in the universe, and yet, knows us, loves us, and has a plan for us, it is almost all we can do to control the overflow of joy that comes from our hearts.

The notion of such knowledge is something that confuses many scholars and theologians, but in all of the complexity of our universe, we find the simplicity of God's love; that no matter how vast and mysterious this universe may be, there is no change in God's love. Though we may feel as insignificant as the grains of dirt that we walk upon, there is an eternal significance that has been placed on our souls by the God who created the cosmos and has loved us and known us before we were even born. How can we not find joy in knowing a God this big who loves us on a level we will never fully understand?

LORD GOD, THANK YOU SO MUCH FOR LOVING ME. THANK YOU FOR GIVING ME A LEVEL OF LOVE THAT I WILL NEVER UNDERSTAND. EVEN THOUGH YOU CREATED THE STARS, YOU KNOW ME AND LOVE ME. REMIND ME TO NEVER FORGET THAT AND ALWAYS BE THANKFUL.

The Balloon Box

**Start a youth out on his way; even when he
grows old he will not depart from it.**

PROVERBS 22:6

Gender reveal parties are becoming a social media phenomenon. It has almost become an expectation after a couple announces that they are expecting. These parties have a natural magnetism for joy. Friends and family gather to not only enjoy each others' company but to also make a statement. Each guest is making a promise with his or her attendance. They are saying to the expectant parents that they will be there. Not just at the party, of course, but they will be there for the raising of the child. They are communicating to the parents that they are not in this alone. Yes, they are the parents, but they are not alone.

One of the most used props at a gender-reveal party is a box that has been filled with balloons that are either pink or blue. An outside party, a trusted confidant, places pink or blue balloons in the box and then the couple opens the box to reveal the color to their party guests. It is a time of joy for all who see those balloons fly out of that box, but really, the color in the box doesn't ever seem to matter. The parents, though they may have their own preferences, don't ever really seem to care about the color inside. They are just happy that there is a color to celebrate and people with whom to celebrate that color.

No matter if it is pink or blue that comes popping out of that box, the couple has a joy in knowing they are not alone. They are not the only ones who are celebrating. They are not the only ones who are making plans. The parents may be thinking of first steps, first words, and first days of school, but there are also more things happening. Grandparents are thinking about future gifts. Aunts and uncles are planning future lessons and the sharing of wisdom. Family friends are thinking of the date nights where they will fill the role of babysitter.

The balloon box is like a party favor, bringing laughter and joy. It's in plain view for everyone to see, but it's so much more than a simple celebration of gender and upcoming birth. It's in plain view to be a reminder that if you were invited, it is because you have been seen as trustworthy. The couple invites someone not because they are loved, but also because they are trusted in having a hand in the raising of their child, regardless of what the gender may be. With that knowledge, there should be recognition of the responsibility that is placed on the guests, but there should also be a celebration of the trust that is shown from the new parents to their guests.

Trust is a special thing; it comes with responsibility, of course, but even more so, it comes with joy in knowing that this trust has been earned in the first place.

LORD, THANK YOU FOR THE PEOPLE THAT HAVE EARNED MY TRUST, AND THANK YOU FOR THE PEOPLE WHOSE TRUST I HAVE EARNED. ALLOW ME TO HAVE THOSE MOMENTS TO BUILD TRUST WITH OTHERS, AND ALLOW ME TO CONTINUALLY WORK ON MY TRUST OF OTHER PEOPLE. AMEN.

The Presidential Suite

**So, whether you eat or drink, or whatever you
do, do everything for the glory of God.**

1 CORINTHIANS 10:31

Ryan has been working the front desk at a five-star hotel for nearly four years. He started his first day wearing a red vest and pushing bronze carts filled with luggage. Now, he wears a fitted suit, stands behind a marble desk, handles thousands of dollars every day, and above all, the greatest honor, he approves reservations for the presidential suite. This hotel prides itself on having a personal touch to every check-in. After someone approaches the front desk, Ryan calls for an attendant to take the guests' bags and guide them to their room, but every now and again, something special happens. Once a month, he'll receive a call—someone making a reservation for the presidential suite.

Whenever this happens, Ryan glows a little. He gets to leave the marble desk and guide these VIPs to their room. He doesn't have to carry bags, but he always does. On the way to the room, he tells guests about special services that the hotel provides: a complimentary taxi service, complimentary room service, as well as a private room reservation to any of the top five restaurants in the city. None of that really matters to Ryan, but he always says it with a smile, not because of the words, or the VIP, but because of the room itself.

When approaching the door, a guest will notice that it is the only door without the need of a key card. It still uses a traditional key. The lock is changed once a year for security reasons, but nevertheless, the uniqueness of this room starts even before you enter the room. After the key is turned and the door is opened, Ryan gets to give a tour of the room. He points out the floor-to-ceiling windows. He discusses how the furniture is one-of-a-kind made by the top carpenters in the world. He shows various pieces of artwork that the hotel has procured over the years. He points out what is special about every single nook and cranny of the suite. The VIP always has a glazed look, but for Ryan, he dreams of hearing these words spoken to him one day. This specific tour is special for both good and bad reasons. Ryan is getting a promotion to being the manager of the entire hotel, but he will no longer be the one giving the tour.

Many times, we often look at new doors as a little scary because we may be comfortable where we currently are. Next steps can always be a little intimidating because it's unknown. That shouldn't keep us from moving. Years later, Ryan would remember his last tour. He would remember that next day. He would trade a marble desk next to the front door for an oak desk in a room that resembles a small library. He would move from the attendant of a front desk to being the top manager of the hotel. This comes with a special perk that he looks forward to every year. Every year, *he's* the one that receives the tour. It is one of his greatest joys during the year. He gets to work, makes sure the hotel is running the way it should, and then, he approaches the front desk, gives his name, and takes his tour.

LORD, ALLOW ME TO BE ABLE TO TAKE STEPS
TOWARD THE FUTURE. I KNOW THERE ARE TIMES
WHERE I LOOK AT MY CURRENT SITUATIONS
AND I MAY BE COMFORTABLE WHERE I AM. HELP
ME TO KNOW THAT WHATEVER PATH YOU HAVE
GIVEN ME, THERE IS JOY ON THE OTHER SIDE.

19

The Little Things

**Everyone who commits sin practices
lawlessness; and sin is lawlessness.**

1 JOHN 3:4

Y ou can always tell it's Saturday in Christa's home because that is her cleaning day. Her family will tell you this title doesn't seem to make sense because the house never seems dirty for long. Even when it is a little dirty, Christa swings into a germ-killing force to be reckoned with. She has a simple rule, "If you deal with the little things, you'll never have to tackle the big things."

For her, that means throwing away a paper plate the moment it's no longer useful. It means folding laundry as soon as it's done drying. It means weeding the garden as little sprouts break through the soil, and according to Christa, it means mopping and wiping down surfaces every Saturday, regardless of whether or not there is actually a mess to clean up. Every Saturday morning, she sends her husband out with the children to go to the park. They are normally gone for a few hours and will return for lunch. She uses that morning to decompress, listen to an audio book, mop the floors, and wipe down counters and tables.

For the past two years, that has become her weekly ritual. Yes, she may be working, but honestly, she just loves having the home to herself. She enjoys having a quiet home, and even more so, she enjoys making everything clean, even if it wasn't that dirty in the first place, replacing the grime with a shine and a clean smell, marked with a lemony scent.

In life, so many of us ignore our issues. Even if we don't ignore them, we'll do our best to play them off as if they are not as bad as they may seem. They are only the "little sins" after all. It may have just been a white lie, or maybe you take a couple of pens from the office, or maybe you've "forgiven" someone, but avoid them as if there has not been any real reconciliation. Whatever it may be, whenever we let the little things slide, they pile up. Think about it . . . the huge mistakes we've made are probably far and few between. After all, we're not jewel thieves or murderers, but when we let a little white lie here or a little gossip there sneak into our lives, they'll pile up if we don't deal with them.

Christa points out the great joy that comes from having a clean floor. I wonder how much joy comes from having a clean conscience.

LORD, REMIND ME TO TAKE CARE OF THE LITTLE THINGS. DO NOT ALLOW THEM TO STAY. PUT IN ME A HEART THAT DESIRES TO TAKE CARE OF THE LITTLE ISSUES SO THEY DO NOT BECOME BIG. AMEN.

20

Cinnamon Roll Breakfast

**Share with the saints in their
needs; pursue hospitality.**

ROMANS 12:13

Andrea has been working in camp ministry for nearly five years. During the fall, she takes care of coordinating with the summer staff, keeps up with accommodations for groups that are visiting during the off-season, and helps in the searching for Bible study materials for the upcoming summer. She is one of those types who always seem to have a smile on her face or a laugh that is always being prepared. Joy is not a difficult commodity for her to attain. When March approaches, she is wrapping up the organization of her recruiting for the summer. When April passes, she is normally organizing training opportunities and collecting a few last-minute staff applicants. Halfway through May, she organizes names with groups based on what she knows of the group so far. Then, when the staffers arrive, she celebrates their arrival by waving a flag at the entrance as the camp director points them to their cabins for the summer. Simply put, Andrea loves camp.

For many of us, we can probably look back on our time at camp and have fond memories of the lake, archery tracks, hiking, and even crafts, but if there's one thing that most of us have distaste for in regards to camp, it is probably the food. No matter how enjoyable the camp experience was, powdered eggs, rectangle pizza, and mashed potato flakes are rarely welcomed. Surprisingly, between the long hours and the lack of pay, the only thing the staff really complains about is the quality of the food.

This, however, is not the case for Andrea. For her, she takes special care to celebrate the kitchen staff. Every morning she comes in and sings her trademark song, "Cinnamon Roll Breakfast! One of my favorites!" It doesn't matter that cinnamon rolls are served every morning. She still sings the song and the kitchen staff loves her for it. When she sits down with the rest of the summer staff, many of them are perplexed over the joy that she shows in singing. Many never understand why she shows so much joy over the same food every day.

Finally after two weeks of listening to her singing, one of the staffers finally asked why she's always so cheery when she walks into the cafeteria for food that is a little less than desirable. Her response was simple, "Our cooks are actually very talented, but it's a struggle to have the same level of quality meet the quantity of fifty staff and hundreds of campers. They know that their food isn't the best right now. They don't need me reminding them. So I celebrate what I love . . . cinnamon rolls."

For many of us, we forget the importance of spreading joy. There are people around us each day that are frustrated with their current circumstances. Instead of reinforcing the negative, maybe you should choose to focus on the positive.

FATHER, I KNOW THAT THERE ARE MOMENTS WHERE
I FOCUS ON THE NEGATIVE. REMIND ME TO FIND
THE POSITIVE AND CELEBRATE WHAT I FIND. AMEN.

21

Kid Glasses

**But to all who did receive him, he gave
them the right to be children of God,
to those who believe in his name.**

JOHN 1:12

At the age of twenty-seven, Ashley was able to reconnect with some family members that lived on the coast. It was about eleven hours from her Kentucky home, but the drive was worth it. It was not that these family members had been long disconnected from her, but after her grandmother had died a few years ago, it had become harder and harder to spend quality time with cousins that she had once seen three to four times a year. This time, however, was different. She had taken off work, gotten in her car, and drove to spend a week with her cousins. It all worked out. Ashley's husband needed to catch up on work and her cousins' husbands had planned to go on a fishing trip the week that she came down. It was going to be like old times, just her and her cousins catching up and reminiscing on old memories. Plus, there was a beach.

When she arrived, she got out of the car, stretched, and walked to the door to be greeted by her cousins. The greeting, however, seemed forced. There were hugs and smiles and even a bit of laughter, but it all seemed like it was a performance. Something about her cousins seemed different. It was not that her cousins had changed or that Ashley had necessarily changed. Simply put, time had altered family relationships to that of mere acquaintances. They had lost the ability to speak to one another as if they knew each other.

Ashley was worried. She felt as if the time had passed for her to be close with her extended family. With the loss of her grandmother, had she also lost her relationships with her cousins? For her, cousin was merely a title. They acted more like sisters when they were all together.

After a long first day, Ashley started having thoughts about leaving early. She was starting to feel like she was becoming a burden to her family. As they were preparing dinner, she walked to the cabinets to find glasses and a smile started to creep upon her face. "Would you girls like me to take care of the drinks?" she asked.

They both agreed, but as they sat to eat, they would find glasses that were so small that the drinks inside could be finished in four or five sips. The three of them erupted with laughter. Ashley remembered that all of the grandchildren were forced to drink from those kid glasses even when they became teenagers. Their grandmother could never look at them as anything other than her grandbabies.

Sometimes it takes making a small connection to develop a meaningful relationship or even bringing life back into one that seems dead. Find connections with those around you. You might be surprised at the kind of joy that can come from such a connection.

LORD, THANK YOU FOR THE LITTLE THINGS.
THANK YOU FOR THE JOY THAT COMES FROM THE
LITTLE CONNECTIONS THAT KEEP US TOGETHER.
REMIND ME TO LOVE THOSE AROUND ME AND
FIND THE CONNECTIONS THAT WILL FOSTER
RELATIONSHIPS THAT WILL LAST A LIFETIME.

Seeking Refuge

**Trust in him at all times, you people; pour out
your hearts before him. God is our refuge.**

PSALM 62:8

There's a small town in Kansas that prides itself on its amount of farmland and the fact that it only has one stoplight. It is a special little town. It is the kind of place where fingers leave the steering wheel to greet passersby. It is the kind of place where people ask how you are as you purchase groceries. It is the kind of place where the way you shake a hand is a form of judgment on your character. Eyes meet, smiles are exchanged, and warmth is displayed from person to person. Few love the small-town life, but few can deny the charm.

Football games are as mandatory as church. The local diner serves as an information hub, and the art of baking is competitive at town festivals. Finding joy in this town is not exactly a major obstacle, but the true worth of the town is found during the stormy season.

Most of the town is filled with homes that come with basements, but there are a few homes in each neighborhood that are not equipped to handle some of the storms that carve into the Kansas landscape. This, however, does not change the attitude that is displayed on sunny days. When storms are announced, the community prepares for it. Phone calls are made—inviting people to seek shelter in exchange for a pie recipe.

Movie nights are held at the local church to keep families calm in the midst of strong winds. Some families even go as far as having what they call "shelter parties" where they invite neighbors to seek refuge in their basement as they play games and laugh with one another in the midst of howling winds.

When tragedy strikes, it is easy for us to get swept up in the winds of chaos. Many of us are very much aware of those emotions. This is not how it has to be. There is a joy that comes from making the best of a stormy situation. When you work with one another in times of frustration, there is a joy that natural flows from that. When we look out for each other, we discover a joy that shows a love for our neighbors and gains the appreciation of those we ourselves appreciate. Think about the love that you show daily. Who is in the middle of a stormy situation that's in need of a little refuge?

FATHER, I KNOW THERE ARE THOSE AROUND ME
THAT NEED MY HELP. ALLOW ME TO RECOGNIZE
THE NEEDS OF OTHERS AROUND ME, AND ALLOW
ME TO CARE FOR THOSE NEEDS. AMEN.

23

Single and Looking

**My dear brothers and sisters, understand
this: Everyone should be quick to listen,
slow to speak, and slow to anger.**

JAMES 1:19

Jessi runs a small sign business on the weekends. Well, technically, it's an online store, but she only works on the creation of signs on the weekends. When she first started, she was only working on projects for family and friends, but now, she has a thriving business and thinking about giving it a full-time focus. She makes yard signs with cutesy little sayings like "Gnome Sweet Gnome," or she creates stained pallets that have been repurposed to hang coffee mugs.

Her best seller, however, is a sign that goes in the laundry room that says "Single and Looking." It serves as a tipped hat to the social media sites where relationship statuses can be as descriptive as one would like them to be. It is a small sign. It is maybe only 7 to 8 inches wide and is made of cut up pieces of pallet wood. It is stained to resemble mahogany and has two clothespins glued to the front of the stained wood. Finally, with playful font, she paints, in black, the words, "Single and Looking." She made the sign to be a cute reminder that a sock is missing its partner.

When asked about what inspired her to make such a sign, she gives a rather amusing response. She admitted to despising doing laundry. It was not because she did not appreciate having clean clothes, but she always hated the prospect of losing a sock. "It was infuriating!" she would admit. "I would lose a sock, and then, I would lose track of the sock that wasn't lost—making both socks lost and me being without a pair. So, I created a sign that remind me of two things: (1) It's just a sock. (2) It's normally only temporary."

How many of us allow little frustrations like losing a sock keep us from maintaining our joy? How often do the little hiccups of the day keep us from actually finding and choosing joy? When these little frustrations pop up, maybe a better tactic is to remember that frustration is normally temporary and not worthy of giving it control over our joy.

LORD, I HAVE ALLOWED LITTLE THINGS TO CAUSE BIG FRUSTRATIONS. REMIND ME THAT THE LITTLE PROBLEMS ARE JUST THAT, LITTLE PROBLEMS. ALLOW ME TO CHOOSE JOY IN THE MOMENTS THAT ONLY SEEM TO OFFER FRUSTRATIONS.

24

Some Assembly Required

**All Scripture is inspired by God and is
profitable for teaching, for rebuking, for
correcting, for training in righteousness.**

2 TIMOTHY 3:16

The most devastating words that some parents can read off of a box is "Some Assembly Required." For many, it seems that there is this innate desire to put together any project without the use of the manual. Many parents have shared stories of trying to do it on their own and inevitably spending more time than was probably required. Assembly instructions of the past were once nightmares—filled with paragraphs of information in various languages.

Now, most assembly instructions come with clear pictures and short sentences that are easy for many to follow. Yet, there is still this aversion to the use of these instructions. No matter how easy these instructions have been made to follow, people still find a way to try and figure it out on their own. Still, there's always that moment where the assembler gives up, throws their hands in the air, grabs the booklet, and puts together the project the way it was written.

There is little difference in our daily walks with the Lord, especially in reading His Word. In centuries past, the Bible was once hard to attain for the general public. One would have to be a scholar in order to actively translate the Greek, Hebrew, or Latin text, and then share that knowledge with people. For many, the only biblical instruction that could be received was from a representative of the church. Now, the Bible has not only been translated into many languages, it has also had sub-translations to communicate the Bible concepts that are either word-for-word translations, or even thought-for-thought, and even though all of these options are in front of us, so many of us choose to try and figure out the Christian walk on our own.

We go to church. We listen to our church staff. We pray. We may even serve, but so many still don't take the time to actually read the Bible. It's always interesting in Sunday school classes or community groups when we hear someone say that they are asking the Lord for wisdom. How often do we hear this question and never think to open His Word? When boxes say, "Some Assembly Required," there is a reason for it. It means the assembler can assume there is probably going to be some list of instructions to follow. When we talk about living a Christian life, we should not be surprised that there is a book that comes with it.

Like that swing set, bookshelf, or desk that came in a box with instructions, we too are a work that is unfinished. God gave us incredible talents, gifts, and insights that allow us to walk confidently with Him daily. But without a little guidance from the Bible, we are just putting together the pieces without any guidance. Take joy in knowing that there is guidance through prayer and fellowship with other Christians, but most of all, we will always find a deeper wisdom in the reading of His Word.

LORD, REMIND ME TO CONSTANTLY BE AWARE OF THE IMPORTANCE OF READING YOUR WORD. WHEN I ASK FOR WISDOM, STIR MY HEART AND MY MIND TO SEEK OUT THAT WISDOM THROUGH THE BIBLE. AMEN.

25

The Great Physician

**He forgives all your iniquity;
he heals all your diseases.**

PSALM 103:3

Have you ever been to the doctor? I suppose a more appropriate question would be about one's reluctance to go to the doctor. Most of us have probably been to a doctor, but even more of us have probably had an unwillingness to actually go and make an appointment. We invent hundreds of reasons in our minds for not needing to go. We say things like: "It's not that bad." Or "I don't have the time." Or "I just need to rest." My favorite one that I often hear is, "I just need to shake it off." There is nothing more wrong with this sentiment.

Whenever we get the sniffles or a bit of hay fever, our attitude is to simply push through the illness in hopes that our bodies will just "get with the program." That's not how our bodies work. That's not how anything works. Whenever the "check engine" light comes on in our car, we all know it's not wise to just keep forcing our cars to putter on like nothing needs to be repaired.

Many of us have had the moment where we finally drag our feet into the doctor's office and admit we need a little bit of help, and most of us can remember a time when the doctor has looked at us and asked, "Why didn't you come in sooner?" The result is always the same. Our medication is a little more expensive than it could have been; our recovery takes a bit longer than it should have taken, and our lives are hindered just a little bit longer than they need to be. That's not the issue though. No matter how much we may hate going to the doctor, there is still a sigh of relief. There is that regained pep in our step simply because we know the sickness has been treated or is in the process of treatment.

In our Christian walk, we all encounter the sickness of sin from time to time. Many of us try and handle it on our own. We assume repentance is simply not doing a certain behavior any more, but it goes so much deeper than that. To deal with sin is to take it to Christ—asking for forgiveness and removing the desire for it in your heart. Like sickness, the longer sin stays, the harder it is to get rid of. Treat the disease of sin, and discover the joy of walking a healthy Christian life with Christ as the great physician!

LORD, I AM SICK. I HAVE ALLOWED MYSELF TO WALK IN SIN. REMIND ME THAT SIN IS A SICKNESS WHICH NEEDS YOUR ATTENTION. REMIND ME TO COME TO YOU IN MY TIME OF NEED SO THIS DISEASE CAN BE REMOVED. AMEN.

26

Dents and All

But God proves his own love for us in that while we were still sinners, Christ died for us.

ROMANS 5:8

Few people ever forget their first car. Especially if it's one they bought with their own money. For Audrey, she was not going to be able to purchase anything too terribly fancy. She had gained a fairly decent amount of money from working in a fast-food restaurant for a little over a year. She had ridden her bike to the restaurant; taking advantage of the free meal provided as a perk of her employment and had even limited going out with friends to only once a month. Still, she was only able to put away two thousand dollars when it was finally time for her to buy a car.

Staring out at the lot, it seemed that she was not going to be able to find anything. All of the used cars were just outside of her price range. She had learned to haggle from watching her father and mother chisel down prices with other salesmen, but she was beginning to worry. Then, in the back of the lot, she saw her. She laid eyes on the car that she would name Bertha. There were a couple of dents. The paint was missing in some parts, and the rearview mirror was hanging off, but other than that, the car was in good condition. The engine and the inner workings of the car were all intact and still satisfactory in their performance. It was simply what the dealership had deemed an "ugly car."

Even though it had torn seats, the cup holder was questionably sticky, and the radio didn't seem to work, the seat belts were secure, the body was made out of sturdy metal, and the mileage was low. Even though it seemed that the car should have been thrown away, there was still a lot of life left in this car. So, after the test drive, without hesitation, Audrey said, "I want that one!"

They argued on the price for a bit, but she was able to walk away with just enough money to repair the seats and put in a new tank of gas. A few years later, this banged-up car would have a new paint job, the dings removed, and the radio working. Audrey saw that this car's journey was far from being sold for parts in a parking lot.

Christ works very similarly. According to the world, we are a banged-up car, but to Christ, He saw a potential to bring about God's glory. He wants us as we are, dents and all, knowing how far from perfection we are. Even though we were miles away from being seen as perfect, He still chose us and loves us, and uses us for God's will each and every day. There is a joy in knowing that even though we have our dents and scratches, God saw a beautiful creation—waiting to be used.

LORD, THANK YOU FOR CHOOSING ME. THANK YOU FOR LOVING ME EACH AND EVERY DAY. THANK YOU FOR LOOKING PAST MY DENTS AND SCRATCHES AND LOVING ME IN SPITE OF THOSE ISSUES AND USING ME ANYWAY. AMEN.

27

Where Are the Boys?

**For you are saved by grace through faith, and
this is not from yourselves; it is God's gift.**

EPHESIANS 2:8

Adam was a pastor in a small town. He was in his mid-thirties and had two young boys who were acclimating to the idea of their dad being a new pastor in a new town. They were like most young boys at that age: rambunctious, adventurous, and just a little defiant. They were, still, good kids for the most part. They were, as their mother puts it, just boys.

In order to get a little bit of control over their rambunctiousness throughout the week, Adam would make little "deals" with his boys whenever they were out of the house. On Fridays, if they had good reports from their teachers, they would go out for ice cream. On Sundays, if they behaved in church, they would get to pick the movie during their "wind-down" time. On Wednesday nights, if they participated, they would be able to have a can of soda on the ride home. Adam was a fan of deals, and as long as his boys followed the rules, he would hold up his end of the deal.

Tuesdays, however, were special days. Tuesday was the day that the family goes to the store together. For Adam's wife, it had become a great example of anxiety at work. For Adam, it was a welcomed challenge to come up with a new deal every week to keep the boys' interest as well as dedication to acting with common sense while they were in the store. One week it might be a toy. Another time it might be a piece of candy. Sometimes it might even mean getting to stay up an extra thirty minutes. The deal for approved behavior, this day, was a little different. See, the boys had privileges taken away. Today's deal would be earning back those privileges. The boys were on their best behavior, but when the time came for them to leave, Adam's wife asked, "Where are the boys?" Adam's face fell—hating the knowledge that he was going to have to be the bad guy.

He walked throughout the store and finally heard his sons, but instead of the sound of laughter and mischief, he heard his sons crying. They had gotten lost, and even though they knew that their father would find them, they were sad to know they were going to miss out on their reward and that their punishment for prior behavior was going to continue. Upon hearing this, Adam simply found his boys, hugged them both tightly, and they went home. There was no punishment, only love from a father.

When we look at our past, it's easy to think about how it will keep us from moving forward. Our past mistakes put us in a place where we feel as if there is nothing more for us, but that's not how God works. He does not look at our past and punish us for our poor decisions. On the contrary, He embraces us and loves us in spite of our wrongdoings. That is the kind of love God gives.

FATHER, THANK YOU FOR LOVING ME IN SPITE OF MY PAST. THERE ARE MANY THINGS THAT I HAVE DONE WRONG AND YET, YOU STILL CHOOSE TO LOVE ME. REMIND ME EACH DAY OF THIS LOVE, AND ALLOW ME TO KNOW YOU MORE AND MORE WITH EACH PASSING DAY. AMEN.

28

Lunch Box Notes

Until I come, give your attention to public reading, exhortation, and teaching.

1 TIMOTHY 4:13

Sometimes, one of the nicest things we can receive is a little note from a loved one. In a world of emails, text messages, and digital posts, the handwritten message conveys that something was special enough to write down. Loving spouses will leave little notes for one another as a brief reminder—conveying the amount of care that went into the writing of each word. Long-time friends might even send a letter in the mail—taking days for someone to receive just letting them know they were simply thinking about them. But even though it is probably the simplest of handwritten notes, there is something special about the lunch box note.

Many children take it for granted but long for them in their boxes once they become older. The lunch box note is special in its own right. Though handwritten letters and messages are sent to convey a message, lunch box notes are sent in containers that should already do the talking. When a child opens up his or her lunch box, they should already be aware of the love that has been given to them. In the box itself, a child finds a sandwich, chips, some fruit, and maybe something sweet. This sustenance should be a message of love in itself. The lunch box note, however, goes a step further. It doesn't necessarily matter what the note says—they all have the same message. They say, "Hey, I did this because I love you, but I had something written down to remind you just how much . . ."

As Christians, we know that Christ died for us. We know that His sacrifice was the greatest sign of love anyone could ever show. Most Christians have this knowledge without ever reading their Bible, and I cannot think of a more sad reality. It's like opening your lunch box as a child, seeing the note that has been written for you, and then tossing it to the side without ever opening it. There is no way you would ever do that.

The Bible was written to convey God's love for you. So yes, you may have the knowledge of what Christ has done. You may know that God loved you so much that He sent Jesus to die for you, but you'll never be able to experience the joy of getting a glimpse of just how much He loves each and every one of us unless we take the time to open the Bible and read about it.

LORD, THANK YOU FOR SENDING YOUR SON TO DIE FOR ME. THANK YOU SO MUCH FOR SHOWING THAT LOVE FOR ME. REMIND ME TO DIVE INTO YOUR WORD AND LEARN MORE AND MORE ABOUT THE LOVE THAT YOU'VE SHOWN AND CONTINUE TO SHOW EACH DAY. AMEN.

29

The Oak Desk

**One generation will declare your works to the
next and will proclaim your mighty acts.**

PSALM 145:4

On the upper floors of an old Manhattan office building sits an oak desk that has served many. They don't make pieces quite like this any more. It is one of those furniture pieces that seems to outlast time. Six drawers with squared brass handles make up the storage for the desk, and an extended surface allows for guests to be able to fill out paperwork with comfort. It even comes with a matching credenza that operates as a filing cabinet for whomever works in the office. The desk itself has been one of the reasons people will deny promotions just so they can stay in their office with this desk.

The head of the company has even argued that such a desk should be in his office, but is always met with resistance because of the fact that it would be difficult to remove it from the office. The desk has been in the office for nearly a hundred years. The old office building has become a bit of a landmark but has always been used for the publishing industry. No matter the position that has represented the office, something peculiar has been kept a secret among those that have occupied this office. If one lies on the floor and opens one of the desk drawers, they will find a message that has been written on the bottom of one of the drawers. The message is a simple one that was written decades ago, "Your work is your legacy, not the desk . . ." and underneath this message is a series of signatures and years next to the names—representing the ones who have worked from this desk and the time they've worked from it.

So many times, we get caught up in the niceties of life that we forget why we were put here. We put our joy in the wrong place. We chase after the nice cars and the fancy clothes so often that we can forget the reality of what we are created for in the first place. We may want the new house with the marble countertops and then forget that the room was to be used to share meals and stories. We may find that expensive mini-van with the heated seats and adjustable cup holders, but shouldn't we focus on having something safe that can get us from place to place?

It's okay for us to have nice things. It is not wrong to appreciate high quality materials, but this is not where our joy belongs. Our joy is found in what we do with these things. Maybe your oak desk is that new refrigerator. Maybe it's that new bedroom suite. Whatever it may be, instead of placing your joy in the material, think about how it can be used to benefit others. Maybe that refrigerator will provide a little more space to serve those who might be in need of a meal. Maybe the bedroom suite can be used for family feeling at home when they come to visit. Putting joy in an object is a shallow endeavor, but putting joy in how that object can be used to benefit others is something that offers depth in understanding of joy.

LORD, I ADMIT THERE ARE TIMES I FIXATE ON THE THINGS OF THIS WORLD. I ALLOW MYSELF TO BECOME MATERIALISTIC AND FIND MYSELF INEVITABLY UNSATISFIED WITH THESE THINGS. REMIND ME THAT THINGS ARE ONLY AS DEEP AS THE PURPOSE GIVEN TO THEM. REMIND ME THAT MY PURPOSE IS FOUND IN YOU. AMEN.

30

Blanket Forts

"This book of instruction must not depart from your mouth; you are to meditate on it day and night so that you may carefully observe everything written in it. For then you will prosper and succeed in whatever you do."

JOSHUA 1:8

Have you ever made a blanket fort? Did you ever make a little hideaway using a combination of pillows and blankets as a child? Chances are that most of us have made such a fort or have witnessed the creation of one. We have seen simple ones that have used a couple of chairs, and some of us have seen elaborate castles using all forms of furniture and boxes as the support. Whatever the style or extravagance may be attached to the fort, there is something that remains the same. There is a little bit of joy when it's actually seen. Even for those of us who have to have our houses in perfect order, there is still that little bit of childish glee when we actually see these tents made from our blankets. No matter what mood we may be in, there is this adoption of childish wonder to our attitudes when we see one.

This wonder does not come from our actual enjoyment of these forts (even though they are a little fun). This wonder comes from reminiscence. It comes from a memory or an emotion that has not been experienced in a long time. We all have these moments. It might be the smell of a certain baked good that brings back memories of a loved one. It might be a song that brings us back to a certain moment. Sometimes, it might even be a piece of clothing that a child wears just like an older relative. The recognition of this feeling is something that is incredibly special. It shows that there was a deeper appreciation for something than we originally anticipated.

Our relationship with Christ is no different. Like seeing a blanket fort in use, sometimes stumbling upon a certain biblical passage can provide a deeper meaning than what we originally remembered. For all Christians, the Bible is a message that constantly evolves. It is something that constantly deepens itself in our hearts each time we take the time to actually study it. Think about your favorite Scripture. Think about the first time it revealed itself to you. Think about how the wisdom of the verse or passage has burrowed deeper and deeper in your heart each time you've read it.

Like the blanket fort, our understanding of Scripture deepens the older we get. As a child, the blanket fort was something that was simple fun. As adults, blanket forts are a symbol of a simpler, purer time. Its meaning has deepened the older we've gotten. For the Bible, a verse might have been something that was special to our ears or eyes, but as we got older, we understood the historical and theological significance of our favorite passages, and that is a joy that cannot be explained.

LORD, ALLOW ME TO DIG DEEPER INTO SCRIPTURE EACH DAY. THANK YOU FOR PLACING SPECIAL PASSAGES THAT HAVE HELD A CERTAIN WISDOM IN EVERY WORD FOR MY LIFE. REMIND ME TO STUDY THESE PASSAGES MORE EACH DAY. GIVE ME A DEPTH IN MY UNDERSTANDING OF YOUR WORD EACH TIME I READ IT. AMEN.

31

Sound Machine

"Do not fear, for I am with you; do not be afraid, for I am your God. I will strengthen you; I will help you; I will hold on to you with my righteous right hand."

ISAIAH 41:10

Jenny has a difficult time falling asleep. To remedy this, Jenny uses a sound machine to sleep. She has gotten to a point where if she does not hear the sound of waves and tropical birds, then actually falling asleep is something that takes a bit longer than she would like. Each night before she goes to bed, she sets her alarm, makes sure the doors are locked, checks her schedule for the next day, and then turns on a little box with prerecorded sounds that go on for a couple of hours until she actually dozes off to sleep. When the sound machine is on, it still takes her about a half hour for her to finally shut off her brain and let the waves carry her off into a deepened sleep. Without the sound machine, she'll toss and turn for a few hours until her body and mind exhaust themselves.

Because of this, Jenny hates to travel. She hates going anywhere without this little machine. She's even been known to drive to destinations that she should clearly fly to just so she can bring this little box. After about a year of this behavior, her husband had just about enough. He did not want his wife to miss out on rest, but she had developed a near addiction to this device. So, for their yearly vacation, he took two weeks in hopes to actually break her from this addiction. They went to a beach that was only a few hours away. When they arrived, the husband admitted that he had "forgotten" to pack her sound machine. Mortified, his wife was determined to go to the store and just buy a new one, but her husband begged her to simply give it a few days without the box. She agreed and to her surprise, with the windows open, letting in the natural sounds of the beach, she would find out that her sound machine was no comparison to the real thing. It was the best sleep she had ever had.

In life, there are so many times where we settle for substitutes. We will go after the lower quality simply because it is easier to attain. Sometimes, that's all a person can do, but many times, you shouldn't just settle for second best. That means actually working for the higher quality parts of life. Fast food might provide sustenance, but is it the same kind of quality as a home-cooked meal? A phone call may provide a connection, but is it the same kind of quality as meeting for dinner? This devotional might remind you of God's goodness and the joy we receive from a relationship with Him, but is it the same quality as actually reading Scripture and spending time with Him in prayer? Don't settle for substitutes—actually spend time with God and His Word. The quality of joy in being intentional with Him is something unparalleled.

LORD, THERE ARE SO MANY TIMES THAT I SETTLE FOR AN APP ON MY PHONE OR A QUICK PRAYER OVER DINNER AND COUNT THAT AS HIGH QUALITY TIME WITH YOU. REMIND ME OF YOUR GOODNESS EACH DAY AND THE JOY THAT COMES FROM SPENDING TIME WITH YOU. REMIND ME TO DIG DEEPER AND SPEND REAL TIME WITH YOU EACH DAY. AMEN.

Recharge

He said to them, "Come away by yourselves to a remote place and rest for a while." For many people were coming and going, and they did not even have time to eat.

MARK 6:31

There's an interesting phenomenon that has been occurring with people of all ages in this new technological era. Every single one of us has learned, for better or worse, the importance of keeping a battery charged on our phones. Some will take their phones for granted and run out of battery before the day is even over. Others will learn the battery's life and adjust to make sure that it lasts for, at least, the majority of the day. Whichever person you are doesn't matter. What matters is the fact that both types of individuals recognize the inevitable need of putting the phone down and allowing it to charge. We can find little ways around this concept. Some of us can sit next to the electrical socket and still use the phone while it charges. Some will even go as far as buying a portable charger that needs to be charged as well. No matter which is done, there is no substitute for simply laying down the phone, letting it charge, and leaving it alone.

It's amazing that so many of us understand this when it comes down to our devices, and yet we will completely forget this reality when it comes down to our own lives. We take on extra hours at work. We give just a little more effort on that project that needs to be finished. We stay up just a little bit later to make sure that the next day has already been planned. Don't get me wrong. There is nothing wrong with hard work. It is one of the best things we can do. I don't believe there is such a thing as overworking, but it should be stated that there is such a thing as under-resting. Many of us push through our days taking care of kids, making sure everyone is fed, and where they need to be when they need to be there and then the only rest we get is when we collapse into our beds only to wake up and repeat the cycle again. This is not the kind of lives we were created to live. We were not made to simply survive. We were made to thrive.

Our rest is important. It is paramount to the joy that we find in life. When we don't take the time to recharge and regroup, we miss out on the joy that can be found in life. Birthday parties aren't as special when you're exhausted. Family gatherings are not as meaningful when you haven't slept, and even spending time with the Lord can seem tedious if you enter that time feeling like you're about to collapse. Simply put, rest, regroup, and recharge. The joy you'll experience with a rested heart will be more than you could ever experience with a tired soul.

LORD, HELP ME REST. I KNOW THE IMPORTANCE OF IT, BUT I ADMIT I HAVE NOT MADE IT A PRIORITY. ALLOW ME TO MAKE TIME FOR REST. ALLOW ME TO BE ABLE TO LET OTHERS KNOW WHEN THAT REST IS NECESSARY. AMEN.

33

The Bus Station

**Then we who are still alive, who are left,
will be caught up together with them in
the clouds to meet the Lord in the air, and
so we will always be with the Lord.**

1 THESSALONIANS 4:17

Have you ever been on a bus before? I'm not talking about a bus for a field trip or riding one home from school. I'm talking about buying a ticket, waiting at a bus station, and riding a bus to a planned destination. Millions of people ride these buses every year for one of two reasons: to save money or the inability to afford a plane ticket. Needless to say, a few unsavory types normally occupy these stations. Many times, people don't even really speak to one another while at the station or on the bus. They simply keep their heads down until they make it to their destination. Still, even with this lack of conversation or community, there are still glimpses of human decency and camaraderie among the travelers.

You see strangers leaning on each other for rest. But nothing exactly replaces the feeling of shared smiles—seeing someone make it to their destination. These travelers can often see the entire country from a bus window. They hop off one bus and transfer to the next. Friendships are fostered on these buses and never discussed again after their arrival, but still, like friends, whenever one traveler gets to view another being greeted at a station, there is a joy that comes from witnessing the greetings given from whomever is picking up the traveler.

For some, it's a reminder of what is to come. There's something special about coming home. The circumstances of one's return don't seem to matter. There is always some level of joy at returning to the familiar—returning to a sense of security and safety. Family is the reminder of that security that we so often take for granted.

With reunion comes a joy like none other. Reunion exists to remind us that even though many of us may spend time apart, the love that is carried between family and friends is something that outlasts both distance and time. God's love for us is the same. Many of us think about the life we live on this earth, and yet, do not even begin to question the love that God has for us. Even though our reunion with Him is something of a mystery, we know the reunion is coming. We know there will be an indescribable joy when being face to face with our loving Father. You notice something about the people that are picked up from the bus station. They never look back. They accept joyfully that it's over and that the destination was always worth the journey.

LORD, THANK YOU FOR GIVING ME A GLIMPSE OF THE JOY I WILL EXPERIENCE WHEN I COME HOME TO YOU. THANK YOU FOR THE JOY THAT COMES FROM BEING REUNITED WITH LOVED ONES AND REMIND ME TO APPRECIATE THE LOVE THAT IS FELT WHENEVER THERE IS A REUNION. AMEN.

34

Cleaning Out Your Desk

**Let your eyes look forward; fix
your gaze straight ahead.**

PROVERBS 4:25

Upon reading this title, one would probably question the validity of such a story being in a book about joy. Some of us have definitely carried out this title in one form or another, and it's never quite felt like a joyful experience. This, however, does not mean that joy is an impossibility. For one young woman, cleaning out her desk was not something that gave her a great deal of excitement. She had made friendships at this desk. She had gained new skills at this desk. She even had a perfect view of the city's skyline that the rest of the office had come to envy, and yet, she was leaving this desk. She was leaving these experiences that had shaped her professionally and personally. How could she be expected to find joy? How could she be expected to even smile in such a situation? The answer is clear. She chose joy. She chose to look at what was on the other side of her current situation.

For this young woman, cleaning out her desk was not the result of a firing or a layoff. It was the result of a new opportunity. She had been given a chance to better herself at a new company with better hours and more money. It was truly a joyous opportunity for her to undertake. Her own boss told her it would be unwise to let such an opportunity slip through her fingers. So, even though she was leaving a place she had come to love and find comfort, she was still in the face of an opportunity that would have more joy on the other side.

For many of us, we are afraid to take steps that might change current situations we had come to know and find comfort. Our heels have dug in; we've planted roots; so the idea of moving on to a new place seems foreign, or even just outright wrong. Sometimes, we confuse happiness for joy. Trust me, there is a difference. Joy means that there is a greater good on the other side of whatever temporary pain we may experience.

Each of us are faced with "clean out your desk" moments every now and again. We are put in situations of having to make a choice between what is nice and comfortable to what could be greater and more joyous than what we could ever imagine. So, don't be afraid to "clean out your desk." Don't allow current pleasures and comforts keep you from moving forward. It may mean there is a potential for suffering frustration in the short-term, but just know there is normally a joy that comes out of that season. There is joy waiting on the other side of suffering for the right reasons.

How many times have you allowed the comforts of your current situations to keep you from moving forward? Are there opportunities around you now that are keeping you from taking advantage of new opportunities?

LORD, ALLOW ME TO NOTICE THE MOMENTS WHEN YOU HAVE CALLED ME TO MOVE FORWARD. REMIND ME OF THE JOY THAT IS FOUND ON THE OTHER SIDE OF CHOOSING TO FOLLOW YOU EACH AND EVERY DAY. AMEN.

35

Happiness or Joy?

"I have told you these things so that my joy may be in you and your joy may be complete."

JOHN 15:11

It's amazing when we come across two words that may have many similarities but the difference is paramount to understanding their meanings. Hunger is something we all have felt, but starvation is something we pray we never feel. Many of us have been surprised, but few of us can truly say we've ever actually been amazed. An issue we often run into in the English language is something I've come to call "natural hyperbole." Simply put, it's where we use words with a magnitude in definition that may not match the actual circumstance we're describing. After all, how many times have we stated that we're "starving," when, in reality, it has only been a few hours since we've eaten? How many times have you heard someone describe an "amazing" feat you've witnessed a thousand times before? We are all guilty of it. Happiness and joy, however, are a little different.

The difference between the two essentially points to the notion of depth. Happiness normally yields itself to the temporary. For instance, think about that pint of ice cream you get on the special days. For some of us, that little bit of sweetness over the weekend is one of the little things we look forward to after a long week's work, but would you consider it a *joy* to get that ice cream?

We all would definitely admit it is something that makes us happy, but to give joy to something so insignificant is a disservice to the word. This does not mean that happiness is bad. There are many things that make us happy that are, in fact, quite good, but think about it for a moment. Most things that bring happiness are superficial and have a shelf life. Joy, however, implies a sense of depth and offers something that is more lasting.

Joy is a word that is meant to be reserved for the things in the world that are more than just temporary. Joy comes from a good marriage. It comes from a calling. It comes from a deep relationship with God. A wedding day is normally coupled with joy because we understand there is the implication of a life that is going to be built between two people. The acceptance of Jesus brings joy because we understand the eternal implications of such a decision. When we use the word, *joy*, we are talking about something much deeper than happiness.

So, when we talk about the notion of happiness, don't think of it as a bad thing. In fact, accept the happy moments as they come. Enjoy them, but don't immediately give them the attribute of joy. After all, the ice cream will melt. The new job still comes with frustrating responsibilities, and the sunny day only lasts until the clouds roll in. Happiness is good for a while, but joy deals more in the realm of the eternal.

LORD, THANK YOU FOR THE HAPPY MOMENTS
IN MY LIFE. THANK YOU FOR ALL OF THE GOOD
TIMES, EVEN WHEN THEY ARE TEMPORARY.
ALLOW ME TO REALIZE THE DEPTH OF JOY.
ALLOW ME TO FIND THAT REALIZATION IN
YOU EACH AND EVERY DAY. AMEN.

36

Be Present

Do not be conformed to this age, but be transformed by the renewing of your mind, so that you may discern what is the good, pleasing, and perfect will of God.

ROMANS 12:2

It has become a point of contention in Sam's household to never put down his phone. He currently works two jobs and has a little bit of contract work on the side that he is doing so he can make enough money to save for his kids' college tuitions. With three little ones running around the house, he has a goal to put, at least, $25,000 in each account by the time they graduate high school. At the rate he is going, he is well on his way to providing that kind of gift for his children before they even make it past middle school.

No one questions Sam's work ethic. He is definitely one of those that puts in the hours and the quality of work rewards him with a generous paycheck. While the average American puts in anywhere between thirty-five and forty hours a week, Sam is normally cranking out sixty to seventy. Every night, however, after dinner, he plops in his favorite chair and plays a couple of mind-numbing games on his phone. His eyes glass over, and he swipes randomly to reach harder and harder levels on the little games that he downloads on his little device.

His kids will run up to him and latch onto his legs and beg him to play with them. They will tug at his pant legs, or even outright sit on his lap and watch him play just so they can spend a little bit of time with their father. Sam's wife allowed the behavior to slide, at first, because his days were long, and he needed that time to decompress. Slowly but surely, though, it started to become a problem. It went from happening only a few times a week to becoming a routine.

Finally, Sam's wife started introducing the idea of "being present." Sam would only play on his phone for one day out of the week. The rest of that time would be dedicated to spending time with the family. Sam was originally not a fan of the concept. He felt like he was having an earned privilege taken away from him. He and his wife argued about the notion for a few days until finally, at breakfast one morning, his daughter came to him at breakfast and sat on his lap. He played with her pigtails and said how much he liked her new barrettes. Her response was sweet, but sobering, "Daddy, I've had these in my hair for a few weeks now." Sam had realized that "being present" was not only a suggestion at a change of behavior; it was a necessity.

In this fast-paced world, we so often allow the little things to pass us by without even a thought until it's almost too late. God gives us these little moments to remind us of the joy He has given us, but often, we are so wrapped up in our own world that we don't even think about the people we love around us. Be present. You may just be surprised at the joy you'll find from the little things.

LORD, REMIND ME TO BE PRESENT. GIVE ME SIGHT IN REGARDS TO THE LITTLE THINGS HAPPENING AROUND ME SO I CAN TAKE NOTE OF THE ONES THAT NEED ME. IT'S IN YOUR NAME I PRAY. AMEN.

Discipline Brings Joy

**No discipline seems enjoyable at the time, but
painful. Later on, however, it yields the peaceful fruit
of righteousness to those who have been trained by it.**

HEBREWS 12:11

Let's be honest for a second. When we hear the word *discipline*, we automatically pair it with a negative connotation. Even though we are fully aware of the benefits that come from living a life of discipline, there is something about the word that makes us automatically identify its negative tendencies. We should, more than likely, associate discipline with a sharpening or honing of one's skills or talents. Instead, we often look at the word and identify a definition that resembles punishment.

That is just not the case. Discipline should be treated with an attitude of joy, not one of despair. Think about all of the things that require discipline: a career, one's health, raising a family. All of these aspects of life require some degree of discipline, but hopefully, we would all agree that these are worthy of one's discipline.

When we think about our careers, that entry-level position was one we would not want to return to, but it is something most of us are grateful for because of the lessons we learned in that position.

Our health is something that is incredibly difficult for us to maintain. Those early morning runs and abstinence from sugary foods are things that some of us would even admit we hate, but the pay off of a strong body is worth the discipline needed to achieve it.

And is there anything with more difficult seasons than raising children? All of those late nights of worrying and praying for their future; all of those difficult conversations about why you should live a life filled with integrity, and even those little moments of picking them up when they fall all seem difficult at the moment, but are so worth it when you get to witness them growing into good people.

Needless to say, discipline is important. It is something that betters ourselves and others. It is the holder of lasting joy and pushes away the notions of temporary pleasure. Discipline, admittedly, is going to be difficult at times, but the payoff for that discipline is always one that is joyous.

LORD, REMIND ME THAT EVEN THOUGH THE ROAD I AM ON MAY BE HARD, IT IS ONE THAT I WILL COME TO APPRECIATE BECAUSE OF WHERE IT LEADS. ALLOW ME TO CARRY ON AN ATTITUDE OF DISCIPLINE AND REMIND ME TO FIND JOY IN THE DIFFICULT SEASONS OF THAT DISCIPLINE. AMEN.

38

The Waiting Room

**I waited patiently for the LORD, and he
turned to me and heard my cry for help.**

PSALM 40:1

One of the hardest things in the world for us to do is wait. In a world where everything can be gained at a moment's notice, waiting is an action that does not seem to make a great deal of sense to us, and why should it? We can have food from virtually any restaurant delivered to us in a matter of minutes. We can order just about anything we could ever think of with two-day delivery. Even the nature of clothing is given to us in a box with a monthly subscription. Let's face it: our world is one that does not exactly foster the virtue of patience.

So, when we think about waiting rooms, they typically stand against everything in which we have become accustomed. Patience is not exactly an attribute we want to have, nor is it a virtue that has been promoted in our post-Amazon age. We see its value, but that does not mean we actually want to have to deal with situations that require patience.

There is nothing that typically requires more patience, however, than having to sit in a waiting room—hoping for positive news to trade off for the patience shown. There is something interesting about waiting rooms. Depending on where they are placed in a hospital can communicate the purpose of the waiting. If they are near the emergency room, then the vibe in the waiting room holds the nature of hoping everything is going to be all right with their loved one. There are sad waiting rooms that communicate a hope for peace—knowing that the pain a loved one is going through has ceased. But in every hospital, there is a waiting room that is hoping for joy.

Families and friends gather in waiting rooms each and every day to celebrate the birth of a child. People excitedly sit in uncomfortable chairs for hours on end as they await the arrival of a new addition. One thing that each and every individual that waits has in common is they never seem to complain about the waiting. They don't ever seem to mention the wait was too long or that the accommodations were not enough. It's almost as if they see the purpose in the patience.

So many of us live with an attitude of inconvenience when we can't get certain things when we want them or the way we want them, but never seem to think about whatever it is that requires our waiting. We always seem to focus on the frustration of the actual waiting. There are going to be times that inevitably require our patience. Instead of focusing on the waiting itself, maybe we should realize that the things in which we are waiting for are things that have purpose in the required patience.

LORD, ALLOW ME TO BE ABLE TO SHOW MORE PATIENCE IN MY LIFE. REMIND ME THAT THERE IS PURPOSE IN PATIENCE. ALLOW ME TO BE ABLE TO FOCUS ON THE THINGS I'M WAITING FOR AND UNDERSTAND THE JOY THAT COMES FROM THAT PATIENCE. AMEN.

39

Tractor Pulls

**We are afflicted in every way but not crushed;
we are perplexed but not in despair; we
are persecuted but not abandoned; we
are struck down but not destroyed.**

2 CORINTHIANS 4:8–9

In the South, there's a magical event called a tractor pull. If you don't know what it is, the secret is in the name. There is a tractor, and it, well, pulls. Families from all over the town build a large engine, cram them into small tractors, or even lawn mowers, and then they pull literal tons of material across a dirt field.

People come from miles and miles to witness these vehicles tow incredible weights. It seems a little anti-climactic in the description, but between the roar of engines and the cheering of audiences, it is something that is often included in many town festivals. There is a joy that is displayed on the faces of children as they see these small vehicles pulling these weights that often are more than three times the size, and at least ten times the weight, of the vehicles pulling them.

These huge events draw an annual crowd that the town has to prepare for, and yet, it seems like something that would not exactly be that entertaining. So why are tractor pulls the kind of events that attract such a crowd? What makes these events hold such a large amount of joy? For those that have gone every year, there is a joy on the improvement that these little tractors have made. At the end of each year, mechanics go back to the barns or garages and improve upon the work they've put into the engines. Sometimes, it may mean adding little parts to the engine that will bring about a better performance. Other times, it can mean the complete rebuilding of the engine in order to gain an entire new outcome. Whatever it may be, it often becomes a family project that lasts throughout the year. When they return, these families are often cheered on for the amount of work that has been placed into the engine.

There's a special lesson that can be learned from these tractor pulls. There are many things in our lives that require a great deal of work. That does not mean these are not worthy endeavors. More often than not, joy seems to come from the amount of work we put into something. When those extra hours at the office bring about a promotion, we find joy from the work. When we walk across that stage to receive a diploma after years of study, we find joy from the mental sharpening. The point is a simple one. No matter how difficult the path may be, there is often a joy that comes from taking that path and seeing it through. Even in the moments when it doesn't go according to plan, we can continue working toward something—knowing that the work is going to be the holder of joy. When the difficult seasons come, don't allow yourself to be discouraged. Instead, acknowledge the joy that will come from the work you have given.

LORD, THANK YOU FOR WORK. ALLOW IT TO BE SOMETHING THAT I LOOK AT WITH JOY. REMIND ME TO LOOK AT THE WORK THAT IS IN FRONT OF ME WITH JOY. ALLOW ME TO UNDERSTAND THAT THE GREAT JOYS OFTEN REQUIRE GREAT WORKS. AMEN.

40

The Crayon Debacle

Consider it a great joy, my brothers and sisters, whenever you experience various trials.

JAMES 1:2

Amy has taken the pronunciation debate to a whole new level. When surrounded by friends, she saw a box of crayons and pointed them out to the room. After pointing them out, Amy was met with perplexed looks and slight smirks. She already knew what was coming.

"Could you say that again?" one of the girls asked.

"A crayon . . ." she responded.

The problem was not with the choice of the word but rather how she was saying it. You see, the word *crayon* has been up for debate for quite a while. It's normally broken down into two camps. It's seen as either cray-ON or cray-UN. Amy, however, had brought a new pronunciation into the discussion. Her pronunciation was almost a blending of both. When she pointed at that sixty-four-crayon container, she identified them as "crowns." Everyone knew she wasn't talking about royal headwear or dental caps. They knew she was talking about the multi-colored wax sticks used by artists both young and old. Nevertheless, there was still that moment of confusion when Amy would say the word. After a few awkward moments had passed, one of her friends finally spoke up and said, "Amy, what are those?"

"Crowns," Amy identified.

A couple of snickers formed, and then finally, laughter followed the snickers. Amy used to get frustrated when people would laugh, but she eventually joined in on the laughter. After the laughter subsided, a friend asked her why she was laughing? After all, most of us hate it when people are laughing at us, but it was her response that gave a little bit of wisdom to the feeling of being the target of a joke. She said plainly, "I would rather be a source of laughter than the source of scorn." Amy had made a decision. She had decided a long time ago to let go of the frustration of pronouncing a word the wrong way and focus on the little bit of laughter that randomly comes whenever she does.

For many of us, we allow little quirks to hold a place of power over our lives. These little issues could allow us to focus on the negativity, but more often than not, we are often offered a chance to choose the positive. For Amy, she could have easily taken the opportunity to get offended over her mispronunciation of a word, but instead, she chose to laugh with others whenever it happened.

For many of us, however, we allow these quirks to upset us. We allow the small issues in our lives to be able to frustrate us to the point where joy can be taken from us, but the reality is we can often choose joy in the moments where most would be frustrated.

LORD, I ADMIT THAT THERE ARE TIMES THAT I ALLOW MY QUIRKS TO FRUSTRATE ME INSTEAD OF LOOKING AT THEM FOR OPPORTUNITIES OF JOY. REMIND ME EACH DAY TO SEE PAST MY FRUSTRATIONS AND LOOK FORWARD TO SPREADING JOY IN THE WAY YOU'VE CREATED ME. AMEN.

41

Time-Out

**Pleasant words are a honeycomb: sweet
to the taste and health to the body.**

PROVERBS 16:24

Fourth grade is a difficult year for many children. You're not exactly old enough to worry about the perils of middle school, but at the same time, you have the expectation to act with some level of maturity. For Mrs. Waddell, she was the enforcer of that maturity. Her primary role was to teach English, Social Studies, and Spelling, but something that seemed to have taken a higher focus over the years was the molding of students from being nervous fourth graders to being prepared middle schoolers. For her, fourth grade should be a year to wrap up any academic misunderstandings before one dove into their first year of middle school. Fourth grade was the year where maturity was fostered.

Because of her educational philosophy, she had become known as a bit of a stickler for rules among the students and parents. The principal would always get calls about Mrs. Waddell's demanding culture that was presented in her classroom, but she ran what he called a "tight ship." Why would he try and fix something that obviously was working?

Mrs. Waddell was a hardened figure and was never afraid to lay down the law when it came down to discipline. Her go-to was always the removal of a student's recess privileges. It didn't matter if you didn't do your homework or forgot to say, "Ma'am." Whether the offense was minor or major, the removal of one's recess was always the sentence issued for the crime. That is until little Brooke Scott waltzed into her class.

She followed all the rules, always turned in her homework, and was always kind to her classmates, but there was a free-spirited nature to her demeanor that Mrs. Waddell had found some level of distaste. When little Brooke finally slipped and forgot to say, "Yes, ma'am," Mrs. Waddell took up the opportunity to take away her recess. Something unexpected, however, happened during recess.

As she sat in the grass—peeling apart little grass blades—Brooke looked up to Mrs. Waddell and said, "You're a good teacher." Unmoved by her statement, Mrs. Waddell responded, "You are still in time-out." The little girl smiled, and said, "I know. I just thought someone should tell you something nice today."

Her statement shook Mrs. Waddell for a moment. She could feel the softest of smiles forming across her face. No one had ever taken the time to compliment her before. No one had ever thought to tell her that she was a good teacher, especially one of her students. Nevertheless, Brooke's kind words struck her, and to this day, little Brooke smiles and waves to Mrs. Waddell as she runs, jumps, swings, and laughs around the playground, and reluctantly, Mrs. Waddell smiles and waves back. It's amazing the amount of joy that comes from a good word.

FATHER, THANK YOU FOR THOSE THAT ARE ALWAYS ABLE TO GIVE A GOOD WORD. REMIND ME TO SHOW KINDNESS THROUGH THE WORDS THAT I USE, AND REMIND ME TO ACCEPT THE JOY THAT COMES FROM THE KINDNESS SHOWN TO ME. AMEN.

42

Jesus Loves Me This I Know

**But I fear that, as the serpent deceived Eve
by his cunning, your minds may be seduced
from a sincere and pure devotion to Christ.**

2 CORINTHIANS 11:3

We all know the song "Jesus Love Me." Most of us have probably either grown up singing it in children's church or have sang it to our children. However you may have sung this song, we have all probably heard it. Though it seems a little obvious to point out, there is a little bit of joy that is felt every time the song is sung. For Caleb, it was no different.

Caleb was in his second year leading worship for a camp he was helping lead. Every staffer had a secondary job along with the building of connections with teens. Some of them were in charge of working in the kitchen. Others were given the responsibility of leading the Bible study. Caleb, however, was given the special responsibility of leading the worship services every night. As a talented musician, he was familiar with all of the worship songs that were on the Christian radio stations and even had an affinity for converting hymns into having a more contemporary sound. One night, however, Caleb felt something leading him to singing a song that was old to the ears but new to the setting. He led with a familiar chord and decided to sing out the familiar rhyme the teens in the room had learned when they were children.

To be honest, most of us would think this was an unwise move. Why would a room filled with teens have the desire to sing such a song? That song, after all, is only for kids, but that's not the attitude that was portrayed. Instead of dismissal or mockery, the song received a loving response. The voices lifted and the teens sang along with Caleb as he led them through the familiar song.

As he sang the last line, he looked out at a crowd of tear-filled eyes. There was silence. Many of the teens started wiping their eyes—admitting the awkwardness they felt from having such an emotional response to such a childish song. To eliminate the awkwardness, Caleb leaned forward and spoke an affirming message to the teens. He said in a broken voice, "You never outgrow simple truths."

In a world where we have made Christian messages so academic and theological, it often feels as if there is something wrong in returning to simple messages, but that's just not the case. In all of the talks on various theologies and philosophies that have come from the deep intentional study of Scripture, many of us often overlook the most powerful message we have come to know—Jesus loves us.

There is a special joy that comes from simplicity. Yes, its message might be one that we all know and can often become trite, but that does not change the fact that each and every one of us are never too old to here a message that is reserved. After all, no matter how old we get, no matter how educated and trained we may become, we never lose the title of "Child of God."

FATHER, I KNOW THERE ARE TIMES WHERE
MY FOCUS IS SOLELY ON THE DEVELOPMENT
OF MY MIND AND MATURITY AS A CHRISTIAN.
ALWAYS REMIND ME THAT NO MATTER
HOW OLD I MAY BECOME I NEVER FORGET
THAT I AM YOUR CHILD. AMEN.

43

Self-Definition

Therefore, if anyone is in Christ, he is a new creation;
the old has passed away, and see, the new has come!

2 CORINTHIANS 5:17

If I were to ask you who you are, what would your answer be? Would you claim your profession? Would you claim your relationship title? Would you maybe even claim your passion? For many of us, we might give our names first, but then, our answers might trail off into what we do actively each and every day, and the reality is that this is the correct response each and every time. We should be defined by our daily identity. For instance, most of us instinctually think of our title as a spouse. After all, every day, we know to whom we are married. For others of us, it would make sense to identify ourselves by our professional designation. That would make sense we are constantly working just about every day, but is this how we are supposed to identify ourselves? Is there not a deeper more meaningful definition to our identity?

The obvious answer you are probably assuming is, of course, "Christian." After all, if you are reading this, there is the assumption you are more than likely a Christian, and yet, if we are truly honest with ourselves, would we give out the word *Christian* first, or would it more than likely fall to sixth or seventh on our list of identities and titles?

The fact is, we sometimes define ourselves by the things we do each and every day. So, because I go to work every day, I might define myself by my job title. Because I speak to my spouse everyday, it would be easy for me to hold the definition based upon my relationship, but is God not more important? Is God not the true holder of our joy? Then, why does our relationship with Him sometimes fall to the lower part of our list?

Well, the hard reality is that we may not be spending the kind of time with Him that we do with our spouses, our jobs, or our passions. God may just be a passing glance that we offer each day, or worse, He may only be noticed when we are in a church building.

This is not an instance in which you are in trouble because of a lack of time with God. This is simply a reminder of the joy that is out there. You may love your job. You may have a rock-solid marriage, but these are all just fractions of the joy that is felt from having an active, living relationship with God.

So, give it a shot. Read your Bible. Pray to God, and discover a joy that can't be explained. Discover the kind of love and excitement that can only come from having a deeper relationship with Him.

FATHER, I WANT SO DESPERATELY TO DEFINE MYSELF BY THE LOVE THAT YOU SHOW ME EACH AND EVERY DAY. PUT IN ME A HEART THAT DESIRES TO BE CLOSER TO YOU. REMIND ME TO READ YOUR WORD EACH DAY AND SET ASIDE SPECIAL TIME FOR YOU THROUGHOUT MY WEEK. AMEN.

44

Night Hikes

**Your word is a lamp for my feet
and a light on my path.**

PSALM 119:105

Have you ever been on a night hike? It is an incredible experience if you ever get the chance to take one. This should go without saying, but never go hiking alone, especially at night. Nevertheless, it has developed into quite the event among outdoor enthusiasts. There is an added sense of mystery to the hike. Even trails that have been taken before can now seem like new worlds when lit by the moon and stars instead of the sun.

It normally takes a little bit longer to go on these trails because of the lack of light. Even if a hiker has been on the trail countless times, there is still the added measure of cautiousness because of the lack of light. In order to combat this, hikers pack flashlights and lanterns to help light the path in front of them. It doesn't mean they can automatically see as far as they can in the sunlight, but it does help for them to at least see a few feet in front of them. Not being able to see the whole path before you is something that should make any of us feel a little uncomfortable, and yet, more and more people are flocking to the outdoors in order to go on these hikes.

Our daily lives are not that different when we think about it. So many of us are on a path that we take steps down each and every day—not knowing what is at the end of it or what is even on the path to some degree, and yet, we still walk it. In a way, all of us are on a night hike. So many of us allow the unknown to hold a debilitating power over us. Even though we know we are to "walk by faith and not by sight," that does not change the fact that we constantly look to the sky and ask God to "give us a sign" or to "show us the way."

That is not how God works; we have been promised to see a few feet in front of us and to trust Him with the rest. Believe it or not, there is a joy in that if you take the time to think about it. We serve a God that has us. We worship a God that loves us so much that even though we may not be able to see the full picture in front of us, we can trust that it is all a part of His plan for our lives. That is the kind of love God has for each and every one of us. How could we not find joy in that?

LORD, THANK YOU. I KNOW THERE ARE TIMES
THAT I DON'T TRUST THE PATH YOU HAVE
SET BEFORE ME, BUT THANK YOU FOR GIVING
ME A PATH TO WALK. ALLOW ME TO TRUST IN
YOU AND RECOGNIZE THE JOY THAT COMES
FROM PUTTING MY TRUST IN YOU. AMEN.

45

The White Globe

"Go, therefore, and make disciples of all nations,
baptizing them in the name of the Father and of the
Son and of the Holy Spirit, teaching them to observe
everything I have commanded you. And remember,
I am with you always, to the end of the age."

MATTHEW 28:19–20

In Alexander's grandfather's study there is a white globe. Most of us know these globes as being multicolored to help find all of the various countries that fill this world. It's actually very rare to be able to find such a globe that isn't colored to some degree. Alexander's grandfather had made a small business for himself in his retirement by making custom globes for people that wanted them. He could make them out of almost any material and color them in almost any color that the buyer could desire. His globes were expensive but many individuals would send him emails with specifications knowing that it was going to be an expensive venture.

Alexander would walk around his grandfather's workshop and see beautiful globes with incredible details. His favorite order, so far, was a solar system he had built for thousands of dollars. His grandfather had even gotten into the business of creating fictional worlds for readers of high fantasy novels. So, it seemed a little bland to find a blank globe that was sitting on his workbench and his grandfather remarking how excited he was to be working on this specific project.

It was definitely large. It was one of the largest ones he had ever seen his grandfather create, but it seemed so basic. The only paint he had placed on it was the lines of the borders of various countries. To Alexander, it was simply a giant white ball. He finally had to ask his grandfather what the fuss was all about for such a project.

In response to his grandson's questioning, he unveiled the stand that would hold the globe. On it was engraved, "Matthew 28:19–20." His grandfather then explained that a church had purchased the globe with specifications to leave the countries blank so they could be painted over the years.

As Alexander's confusion grew, his grandfather explained that the purpose of the globe was to remind the church of their calling to "Go." With every missionary they sent or sponsored, they would fill in the country with the color to which they were spreading the gospel. For Alexander's grandfather, he only charged them for supplies—it was still an expensive venture, but he believed it was his joy as a Christian to be able to participate in such an endeavor.

Many of us forget that the joy of knowing who God is comes with the charge of spreading His name to all the nations of the world. Is it really that much of a charge? When you find out good news, isn't our first instinct automatically to share it? It may be a charge, but it is definitely a joyous one.

LORD, I AM SO GLAD I KNOW YOU. I AM SO GLAD TO KNOW THE GOOD NEWS OF YOU SENDING DOWN YOUR SON TO DIE ON THE CROSS FOR ME. REMIND ME TO SPREAD THIS KNOWLEDGE TO OTHERS. ALLOW THE JOY OF KNOWING YOU TO BE SOMETHING THAT IS SPREAD TO ALL OF THE NATIONS. AMEN.

46

Lights Out!

**In vain you get up early and stay up late,
working hard to have enough food—yes,
he gives sleep to the one he loves.**

PSALM 127:2

We all know what this phrase "Lights Out!" means. We've heard it in our homes when we were children. We've heard it on camping trips or on family vacations. Some of us have maybe even said the words ourselves. "Lights out!" has a definition that is understood without being communicated. It means, "Go to sleep," "Be still," or "Get some rest." According to some parents, it means, "Lie down and be quiet." This little phrase, though, is always said with the same level of authority. It is given with the same tone that would come with a command. Why is this? Why is there this level of authority given for something that should be objectively a good thing? Well, as we all have come to know, children rebel against rest.

Sleep is not something they want to readily happen. For them, they feel as if there is some part of the day they are going to miss, as if there is an adventure that is going on while they rest. It's one of the main reasons why taking a nap is always either a command or a negotiation. Let's face it. Children just don't want to sleep. But are we really that different?

Think about it. How many of us work long hours when we don't necessarily have to or stay up for a couple of extra hours to finish that next episode? How many of us have said, "Yes!" to something when we know we already have so much on our plates? How many of us have agreed to go and spend time with friends when we know we haven't even had time to recharge our batteries? Does it ever feel like we need someone just to pop in and tell us, "Lights out!"? Whether or not we want to admit it, we run ourselves into the ground most days. We push and push until we exhaust ourselves and our bodies and minds wear out. This is not the way we were called to live. We were definitely meant to work hard, but we also need to rest.

This is not an invitation to living a life of laziness, nor is it an excuse to sleep through one's responsibility. Instead, it is an opportunity to experience the joy of rest. Allow rest to come every now and again. Don't push past it as if it's not important. Find little ways to find rest. Take a moment to look in the mirror and say, "Light's out!" The person you see just might be in more need of rest than they'd like to admit. Simply put, work hard. Accomplish great things, but take time for your mind, body, and soul to rest. You may be surprised at the joy that comes from it.

LORD, I AM SO TIRED. THERE ARE SO MANY THINGS I HAVE TO ACCOMPLISH, AND I FEEL I JUST DON'T HAVE THE TIME TO REST. FATHER, GIVE ME TIME TO REST. REMIND ME TO FIND THAT TIME, AND ALLOW ME TO PLACE MY REST IN YOU. AMEN.

47

Joy Thieves

**"A thief comes only to steal and kill and
destroy. I have come so that they may
have life and have it in abundance."**

JOHN 10:10

Think about a time when your joy has been stolen. We can probably all think of a time when someone has taken our joy from us. We all know the culprits. They are the holders of sly comments, disparaging remarks, condescension, sarcasm, rudeness, and even the subtlest facial expressions. These individuals are called joy thieves. They are not brutes that break into our hearts and thrash about our emotions then walk away with the joy they can grab, nor are they exactly cat burglars—cleverly sneaking into our hearts and stealing valuable pieces of that joy. They are more like con artists. They waltz into our lives and convince us to give them our joy. Simply put, we allow them to have our joy.

What a statement! People who upset us are not the ones to blame for our stolen joy? That's right! These individuals only prey on those who they know will willingly give up their joy and trade it for frustration and anger. As difficult as it is for us to admit, it's our fault for allowing our joy to be taken from us. This begs the question. If it is our fault for having our joy taken from us, why does it happen so often? Why would we ever allow someone to have that kind of power over us?

The sad reality is, there are too many reasons to count. Maybe they are a loved one who we want to approve of us. Maybe they are an employer who has an opinion of our work that we value. Maybe they are a friend we want to please. Whoever they may be, there are people who have the ability to just waltz into our hearts and ask for our joy and, for whatever reason, we just hand it over. We place our joy in them.

Sometimes these people misuse our joy on purpose; sometimes it is completely unintentional. We shouldn't be upset with these individuals. Joy is something that is only reserved for those that should hold the deepest kind of trust. It's the reason why divorce and family strife hurt as much as they do. It is because these are appropriate areas to place our trust, even though they have the possibility of letting us down.

I know what you're thinking. Where's the good news? When are we going to get to the actual joyful part? Well, the secret has already been stated. Where are you putting your joy? Are you placing it in your relationships with people, or are you finding your joy in God? It is not necessarily a bad thing to put our joy in people we love and trust, but there is a joy like none other than the one we place in God and our relationship with Him. Don't give people the kind of joy that was meant for God. Give that joy to God and find a love and joy that is untouchable by those around you.

LORD, I CONSTANTLY ALLOW PEOPLE AROUND ME TO STEAL MY JOY. I WILLINGLY GIVE IT TO THEM. REMIND ME THAT IT IS YOU WHO SHOULD HOLD MY JOY. REMIND ME THAT WITH YOU THERE IS A JOY UNLIKE ANY OTHER. AMEN.

48

Chess with Dad

For the vision is yet for the appointed time; it testifies about the end and will not lie. Though it delays, wait for it, since it will certainly come and not be late.

HABAKKUK 2:3

Have you ever played chess? It is a rather simple game but the way one plays has limitless possibilities. There are books that are hundreds of pages long that discuss different kinds of strategies and different tactics one can use in order to make himself a formidable player. For Sarah, there was not a more formidable opponent than that of her father. He was a man of mystery whenever he played the game. It is not that he was an incredibly complex individual. In fact, his day job was working in a factory—constantly tinkering and repairing various machines in the building. He was a mechanic, but the man was nearly unbeatable in a game of chess. Out of the fifteen years that Sarah had played with her father, she could only remember a couple of times when she had actually beaten her father, and she will also be quick to tell you that each of those instances were merciful victories.

Nevertheless, Sarah was determined to figure out her father's strategy. In one game, it seemed like she was going to win. She could spot a checkmate in four moves if her father continued down the path he was going. She contained her excitement as to not alert her father. She moved her rook in front of her father's king.

"Check!" she exclaimed.

Her father grinned and moved his bishop to take her rook. "Bishop takes Rook. Checkmate," he said.

She was furious. How could she have forgotten about his bishop? It had just been sitting off to the side the entire game. In fact, she could not recall her father moving the piece once. Her head hung low—breaking down the game in her head. She could not get over how she had forgotten such an obvious move. Her father, however, gave a hint to his strategy. He kissed her on the head and whispered, "Just because a piece has not been used does not mean that it's useless."

There are so many times that we feel like the bishop in this specific match. We feel that because we have not been put to work for something, it must mean we are without use. This is just not the case. God has a plan for you. Just because you cannot see how the plan is moving does not mean you do not have a part in it. Be patient and take joy in knowing that God will use you for His glory!

LORD, GOD, USE ME AS YOU SEE FIT. ALLOW ME TO BE PATIENT IN THE MOMENTS WHERE YOU CLEARLY HAVE ME WAITING. REMIND ME TO BE PATIENT WHEN I SEE THOSE WHO ARE MOVING AROUND ME AND I FEEL AS IF I'M STUCK. REMIND ME THAT THERE IS A PLAN, THAT YOU ARE GOD, AND I AM NOT. AMEN.

49

Big Boy Shoes

I am sure of this, that he who started a good work in you will carry it on to completion until the day of Christ Jesus.

PHILIPPIANS 1:6

Danny has a slight obsession. It is not a dangerous one nor is it an actual addiction to something, but Danny still has a bit of a fixation with his father's shoes, a specific pair actually. He does not care for his father's tennis shoes, nor does he really care about his slippers, and he's quick to tell you how ugly his father's loafers are, but there's something special about what he has dubbed as his father's "big boy" shoes.

They are light brown dress shoes that are still kept in the box and are only worn for special occasions, important business meetings, and any time his father wears a blue suit. Danny idolizes his father, but there is something that always seems to stand out about him when he wears his "big boy" shoes. He seems to walk with a little more pride. His back is straighter. His smile is just a little bit wider, and when he comes home from wherever he's been, he always seems to have had a better day when he's worn these special shoes.

Because of this, Danny started begging for his own "big boy" shoes. He wanted to be what he called "confident," just like his dad. When it looked as if he was not getting his own "big boy" shoes, he decided to take matters into his own hands.

One morning, as his father was getting ready for church, Danny decided that he would wear his father's shoes. As his father rounded the corner, he asked his wife if she had seen his brown shoes. Instead of finding his wife, he would find Danny—dressed in his church clothes and wearing shoes that were at least twice the length of his feet. His father smiled at the sight and asked him what he was doing wearing his "big boy" shoes. The boy's response struck his father. Danny looked at his father lovingly and said, "I can't do everything you do, but I can at least wear your shoes."

There are so many times that each of us assume because we can't live a life exactly like Christ's then it must mean that living a Christlike life is impossible. That is just not the case. Living a Christlike life simply means doing one's best to live a life according to His example. Because so many of us realize the fact that we cannot come close to that level of perfection, we just assume any attempt is one that will be in vain, but that's just it. Jesus did not call us to be perfect. He did not call us to walk a narrow path without ever stumbling. That should be something that fills us with joy. We are not called to be perfect, we are called to simply follow. So, put on your "big boy" shoes and walk—knowing that the steps don't have to be perfect, just follow the path laid out by our Father.

LORD JESUS, I THANK YOU SO MUCH FOR THE SACRIFICE YOU HAVE MADE FOR EACH AND EVERY ONE OF US. I KNOW THERE ARE DAYS THAT I GET SO FIXATED ON THE NOTION OF LIVING A PERFECT LIFE, AND I KNOW THAT ISN'T RIGHT. REMIND ME EACH DAY THAT YOU HAVE NOT CALLED ME TO BE PERFECT, BUT JUST TO FOLLOW YOU. AMEN.

50

Literally Everything

. . . giving thanks always for everything to God
the Father in the name of our Lord Jesus Christ.

EPHESIANS 5:20

Jenny literally thanks God for everything. That's not a drastic misuse of the word, *literally.* She legitimately thanks God for just about every single thing in her life. As a child, her parents would have her say the blessing before meals because it was cute to hear her thank God for toast and various condiments, but as she grew older, it became tiresome to hear her thank God for every single item that was on the table. Still, Jenny never lost her ability to constantly give thanks to God.

She was thankful in the good times and the bad. She was thankful when she got a promotion last year, and she's even thankful when she's stuck in traffic. It's a bit of a perplexing thing for people to witness. After all, who can be this thankful in every single moment?

For Jenny, she's quick to tell you that being thankful is a daily choice. It is one that requires faith. For her, she knows how easy it is to be thankful when things are all going well, but it is an even greater challenge to have a thankful spirit in the moments that don't go according to plan, but her logic for having a heart of gratefulness is simple. She simply has found that every situation has something for which we can be thankful. For her, it's merely an exercise in focus.

The reality is that so many of us choose to focus on the negative instead of focusing on the positive. When we are late for work because of a wreck, we forget to be thankful that we are the ones who didn't have or cause the wreck. When we get passed over for that promotion, we forget to acknowledge that the promotion might have a level of promotion we may or may not be ready to handle. Even when our meal comes out the wrong way at a restaurant, we don't admit that it's an easy fix and we're the ones sitting in an air-conditioned room and not in a hot kitchen. The fact is, we have so much to be thankful for.

When it comes down to joy, it's all about our focus. Yes, there are definitely moments that are not going to go according to plan, but that does not change the fact that there is always going to be something to be grateful for in *literally* every situation. Sometimes it's easy to focus on the negative. Discover the joy that comes from choosing to see the positive.

LORD, I KNOW THERE ARE TIMES WHERE I AM GUILTY OF NOT LOOKING ON THE BRIGHT SIDE. I KNOW I OFTEN FORGET TO FIND A THANKFUL ATTITUDE WHEN THE TIMES ARE TOUGH. REMIND ME TO LOOK DEEPER AT THE FRUSTRATING MOMENTS IN LIFE AND FIND THE POSITIVE IN THE NEGATIVE. AMEN.

51

Shhh . . .

**Very early in the morning, while it was still
dark, he got up, went out, and made his way to
a deserted place; and there he was praying.**

MARK 1:35

Let's be honest. We live in a loud world. Between the chimes of notifications from our phones, the honking of other cars on our commute, and the yelling of our kids as we maintain the house, we become incredibly aware of just how loud our world is. It is not something that is discouraged, either. On the contrary, televisions are sold with multiple sound capabilities based on the speakers you buy with them. The roar of an engine is what one uses to point out the strength and power of one's vehicle. Even movie theaters, which were already loud, now come with rooms that are lined with speakers to make the audience feel as if they're actually *in* the movie.

Silence is a commodity that is not appreciated. Even in offices where work is meant to have a focus, they are filled with white noise machines that allow us to work in an acceptable level of sound. Most of us cannot even sleep unless there is a fan that has been turned on. Let's face it. We like our noise. In fact, if we were honest, we could probably admit that we are almost uncomfortable when noise is absent.

And yet, silence has so much to offer. Whether we like it or not, silence is actually good for us. It may give us some level of discomfort at first, but there is a point to that discomfort. Think about your "quiet time," for instance. How often do you pray to God while the world is whirring around you? Do you ever try and squeeze Him in between songs on the radio? Do you ever think that you can cram in the reading of His Word while the television is blaring or the kids are running around the house?

I know that we might be focusing on the audible kind of noise, but what about the noise of a chaotic life? Do you try and find a few moments of prayer on your way to work and count that as a rich time that's been filled with God? How about the reading of His Word? How often do we try to just give Scripture a skim while trying to make sure the kids are going to bed?

Sometimes this is all you can get. That's totally understandable. The point of this is not to scold you for missing deeper moments. The point is to move you toward joy. There is joy in silence. When we remove our distractions, we are able to actually dig deeper into our relationship with God. We are able to read His Word more clearly. We are able to pray with a greater level of focus. Don't miss out on the joy of knowing God deeper. Get rid of the distractions. Get rid of the noise and come to know Him better in the silence.

LORD, I KNOW I LIVE OUT A LOUD LIFE. I KNOW
THERE ARE THINGS THAT I NEED TO WORK ON
EACH AND EVERY DAY. ALLOW ME TO PUT THOSE
THINGS TO THE SIDE FOR A FEW MOMENTS
TO GET TO KNOW YOU BETTER. AMEN.

52

The Matchstick

This is the message we have heard from him and declare to you: God is light, and there is absolutely no darkness in him.

1 JOHN 1:5

There's a physics teacher in rural Texas that performs simple experiments for his class that have mind-bending implications. His experiments are never expensive and are never outside of their understanding in the implementation, but still, he has given a couple of lessons that have left the realm of science and moved more into the realm of poetry.

One afternoon, they started their study of light. He had gotten out a crystal prism and shined light through it to show all of the visual elements of refracted light. He brought out an angled mirror and showed the concepts of reflected light, but what he loved the most about the general lesson on light happened around the concept of a matchstick.

He had the kids turn off the lights. He pointed out the reality of darkness. It was a classroom on the interior of the building so there were no windows to allow any light into the room. In a sense, the students got a taste of total darkness. He still continued to speak to the class. He explained that there was such a level of darkness in the room that even once their eyes adjusted to the darkness, there still were going to be major issues of being able to see anything at all. That was until he lit a match. When the match was lit, every eye that was lost in the darkness focused on the front of the room to look upon the light the flame was producing.

As the match went out, he lit another and asked them to slowly turn in a circle. Though it was faint, this small flame had produced enough light that the students could see the objects in the room. The teacher asked, "Does anybody notice anything about this match?" A student raised her hand and said, "We block the light because of our shadows. There is no light in our shadows." The teacher smirked as he lit another match and said, "You could also say there is no darkness in the light."

The students didn't understand until the teacher turned on the lights. He picked up another match and asked the kids to come forward with their phones and put the flash on their cameras. He lit the match and asked the kids to take as many pictures as they could. When the students looked at their pictures, they found out they could see the shadow of the teacher's hand and of the match, but they could not see a shadow for the flame. As the teacher noticed his students' wheels turning, he closed the lesson by saying, "The flame is simply a light source, there is no shadow for light."

LORD, THANK YOU FOR BEING THE LIGHT IN MY LIFE. THANK YOU FOR NOT HAVING ANY FLAWS AND THANK YOU FOR BEING THE PERFECT PART OF MY LIFE. YOU ARE WITHOUT DARKNESS LORD, AND ALLOW ME TO SHARE THE LIGHT THAT YOU GIVE SO FREELY. AMEN.

53

Little Messages

Therefore encourage one another and build each other up as you are already doing.

1 THESSALONIANS 5:11

People often minimize the impact a little note can have. Because of this misinterpretation of a little note's worth, many of us often disregard them altogether—never taking the time to write one out in the first place. Though these little messages may seem insignificant, they often carry the same weight as the discovery of a diamond hidden in the midst of coals.

So many of us constantly deal with the frustrations of daily life. We are constantly sifting through the dirt and rock of our daily responsibilities that we often feel that is all there is for us, but a well-placed and well-timed message can make all the difference in the world.

You've been with the kids all day, and nap time has shifted to the realm of fantasy than that of reality. You've worked on a specific project at your work, and it just feels as if it is never going to end. Maybe you've been on the road for a few hours and just hit an unexpected traffic jam—erasing the notion of making it home on time. Whatever the case may be, we've all been in situations where the day has grown harder and more difficult without any conceivable reason for it. For many of us, we would assume the remedy to these days is the removal of the hardship itself, but sometimes that is just not a possibility for us.

More often than not, we just need a reminder that everything is going to be okay; that we are going to make it through this hardship.

How do we do this? Well, believe it or not, a little message can make a big difference. A short note can go a long way. When our little angels are not acting so angelic, a little note praising our parenting can shift our attitude with our kids. When work has got us bogged down, an email discussing one's thankfulness for us can reenergize us to take on the day. Whatever the struggle, a loving message can change the most difficult of situations.

That's not all. The more care that goes into a note, the better it will be. Yes, a text message or a phone call is fine when that's all you can do, but there's something about an actual written note that stands out. Digital messages are often those that are thrown together with a few taps of a keyboard, a click of a mouse, or a swipe of the thumb. They often communicate an "I didn't have time" mentality. Written notes show a little more care. They show that we went out of our way. They show that we lost a little bit of time to communicate a special message for a special person.

So, get out there and take on the day. Remember the power of a little message and the difference it can make for those who are struggling through the obstacles of their daily responsibilities.

LORD, THANK YOU FOR THE LITTLE MESSAGES OTHERS HAVE GIVEN ME. THANK YOU FOR THE POWER OF A GOOD WORD. REMIND ME TO CARE FOR THOSE IN THIS WAY, AND REMIND ME TO NEVER FORGET THE POWER OF A LITTLE MESSAGE. AMEN.

54

Welcome Banners

Therefore accept one another, just as Christ also accepted you, to the glory of God.

ROMANS 15:7

Welcome banners have become a bit of a trend in churches. You've probably seen them. They have metal bases and large sheets weaved together by some form of plastic thread. They are pulled from the base and clipped on a metal rod like some kind of scroll. On the banner are customized messages to guests that are visiting. They point to where to get information or point to social media or even talk about how to get involved in a church's ministry. Churches all over the county have started using these banners in hopes to have eye-catching information that will implore guests to return. Individual churches have spent thousands of dollars on these banners, and yet, the effectiveness of these banners is not necessarily guaranteed.

Why is this? Why would a company not guarantee the effectiveness of a product like banners? The fact of the matter is that the banners may be there to provide a welcoming atmosphere, but churches are still very much in need of welcoming people. Churches, still, make the mistake of looking at a supplemental material as the main provider for a need.

So many of us are guilty of this mentality when we are a little honest with ourselves. We trick ourselves into thinking that the substitute is enough to satisfy the actual need. We think we'll win "lawn of the month" by hiring a teenager to do yard work for twenty dollars when we should be doing the work ourselves. We think that a weekly phone call to a loved one will count just as much as spending intentional quality time with them. This one is a little awkward, but we go to church, hear a sermon, and allow that to count as the same as actually spending time reading the Bible or intentionally praying.

What do we lose with substitutes? Well, we lose the opportunity for real joy. Think about welcome banners for a moment. Many times, we expect them to give out the information when in reality, there is a deep need for connection. Instead of just standing behind the welcome desk—hoping the sign will do the trick—smile, shake a hand. Have a conversation and discover the joy that comes from a real connection. Don't settle for the substitute. Go after what is real in life and discover how the substitute doesn't even come close to the real thing.

LORD, I KNOW I HAVE BEEN GUILTY OF SETTLING FOR THE SUBSTITUTES IN LIFE WHEN WHAT I REALLY NEED IS SOMETHING GENUINE. REMIND ME TO NOT SETTLE FOR SUBSTITUTES AND TAKE HOLD OF THAT WHICH IS REAL. AMEN.

55

If These Walls Could Talk

"As for me and my family, we will worship the LORD."

JOSHUA 24:15

Many of us have heard the phrase before. It's normally said in a home that has seen "a lot of life." This form of personification is something that is felt by many who walk into an older home. There's something supernatural about walking into a home and feeling the kind of emotion that is exuding from the walls. For some, walking into a home can, sadly, mean pain. A home could have housed arguments and frustrations and even abuse. The walls, somehow, hold those emotions even years after the pains have been dealt. There is sadness in that, but there is a joy like none other when we walk into a home that has been filled with love.

We all know the kind of homes I'm discussing. For some of us, it's a family who has had weeks filled with family game nights, laughter at dinner tables, and loving responses during difficult moments. We know when a house has been soaked in prayer and the reading of Scripture. You can feel when God is a major part of the household. We all know we are supposed to be hospitable, but there is something extraordinary about a home that communicates a warm environment on its own. People see pictures of the family on the walls, or they notice that a Bible is not covered in dust and looks actively used. They notice when the family is talking to each other naturally and not putting on a show for guests.

When a home is filled with these kinds of sights on a consistent basis, it becomes obvious to all of those who come into the home. When a home is filled with the joy of knowing God, it is evident. It makes a statement. It says that this home is one that serves, prays, studies, and above all, loves. Joy is an outflow of our love of God. Our homes should have that outflow crash against their walls in the best of ways. Our walls should be saturated with prayer. Our time spent in the home should be a place that is safe, a place that is secure, a place that is so evident of God's presence in the home and in the lives of those who live there. Joy comes from that. Joy comes from knowing God is the Lord of our lives. That includes where we live just as much as it focuses on how exactly we live.

Take a moment and look at the walls in your home. What would they have to say if they could speak? Would you find joy in what you would hear? Would you want their messages shared with guests? There is a love and joy that is communicated to all that come into your home. Before you focus on what they would hear, though, take time to focus on the joy you can put in those walls by worshiping and serving God.

LORD, I KNOW THERE ARE MOMENTS WHEN I DO NOT LIVE ACCORDING TO YOUR WILL. I KNOW THAT SOMETIMES, I DO IT FROM THE COMFORT OF MY HOME. ALLOW ME TO LOOK AT MY HOME AS A BLESSING YOU HAVE GIVEN AND WITH THAT GIFT COMES A RESPONSIBILITY TO KNOW YOU DEEPER AND SERVE YOUR KINGDOM. AMEN.

56

Block Party

There's a church in Tennessee that has become famous throughout the neighborhood for their yearly block party. A member that owns a restaurant provides burgers and hot dogs. Another member has access to a few bouncy houses and will bring those as well. The church will place money to the side and provide games and refreshments for all who decide to come. It is their own little fall festival that they have offered to any who want to come. People from all over the neighborhood come to the church and participate in the event.

For the kids, they enjoy all of the little games and inflatables that occupy their time for hours on end. For the parents, they enjoy the good food and conversations that come from going with family and friends, but for the pastor, he loves the event for his own reasons. He loves every moment of the event because of his view from the "connection" tent. In the connection tent, you sign up for raffles for big prizes, can handle any cuts or scrapes a child may get from falling on the pavement of the parking lot, or even look at the sign up to see if someone is at the event already or not. Whatever the case may be, the pastor loves it because, frankly, it's what you have to go through in order to get to the actual event.

He uses that time to shake hands and say hello to familiar faces, but that is not his purpose for being there. He's not looking to get new members or visitors from the event (although that would be a plus). On the contrary, you can find the pastor next to a table that says, "Can I pray for you?"

Surprisingly enough, you'll get a few every year who wander over toward that table and seek the counsel of a pastor. Some of them are always one of the members of his congregation, but the purpose of that specific table is for the one who doesn't necessarily go to the church. He always stands nearby—looking for the lost sheep who are in need of a kind word, a nugget of wisdom, or just a simple time of prayer. Whatever the case may be, the table's purpose is one to remind those who come to it of the love and joy that come from knowing who God is.

In life, sometimes it's not the good times that remind us of joy. Sometimes it doesn't matter how much "fun" is around us. Every now and again, we just need a kind word from a kind face to remind us of the joy in life and the joy that comes from loving an all-loving God.

LORD GOD, SOMETIMES I LOOK FOR JOY IN THAT WHICH IS FLASHY, AND IT IS SO OFTEN NOT ENOUGH. BE WITH ME AS I GO THROUGHOUT MY DAY AND REMIND ME OF THE JOY THAT COMES FROM KNOWING YOU. AMEN.

57

Gumball Machine

**"If you remain in me and my words remain in you,
ask whatever you want and it will be done for you."**

JOHN 15:7

I've never exactly understood gumball machines, especially because they are always seen in grocery stores. In fact, I would wager that, outside of the rare doctor's office or car dealership, they are almost exclusively seen at grocery stores. Why point this out? Well, to be completely transparent as to why this seems so illogical, a shopper can find everything that is sold in the gumball machine at the actual store. Frankly, they can have them fresher and can buy more at a cheaper unit price. And yet, gumball machines are thriving, or at least, they are not going anywhere.

Have you ever seen how gumball machines are treated? The candy is changed out only when the machine is out of candy. It costs a quarter only to get one piece of candy, and children with unwashed hands and snotty noses stick their hands up the slots in order to scrape candy gunk off of the sides in order to get just a little bit more. Gumball machines are absolutely disgusting. Still, children beg their parents for extra change in order to get a piece of candy.

Why do these machines still exist when we know these little disturbing facts? How do children, and some adults, fall for the allure of the gumball machine when, in the back of their minds, they are fully aware they could just buy the same product from the store? To be honest, I think it has something to do with the instant gratification of putting something in and immediately getting something out. As much as we hate to admit it, we all have our own version of the gumball machine. All of us have even been guilty of treating God as if He is the keeper of the gumball machine over our lives.

Be honest with yourself for a moment. Have you ever prayed to God and immediately expected a response the way you interpreted it? Have you ever been in that moment of looking for a job and asked God to answer a prayer? How do you feel when you don't get a response that moment? Frustrated? Annoyed? When have you sought God out for wisdom and then been angered when knowledge has not simply landed on your head? The sad truth is that many of us have had a gumball machine mentality at least once. This is not how we were called to live out our lives. Treating God like a gumball machine is not something that provides joy. More often than not, joy comes from patience. Like telling a child he can have something better instead of settling for instant gratification, God allows us to realize that the best things in life are the things worth waiting for.

LORD, I KNOW THERE ARE TIMES WHEN I AM IMPATIENT. REMIND ME THAT THERE IS JOY IN KNOWING THERE IS A TIME AND PLACE FOR EVERYTHING ACCORDING TO YOUR WILL. AMEN.

58

S'more Time

**But grow in the grace and knowledge of our
Lord and Savior Jesus Christ. To him be the
glory both now and to the day of eternity.**

2 PETER 3:18

S'mores have now become necessary accessories to the campfire experience. One of the first questions that is often coupled with the notion of gathering for a campfire is centered around who is bringing the graham crackers, the marshmallows, and the chocolate bars. They are a unique treat, and they have become a part of the camping experience ever since their creation. Simply put, if there's a fire, there's a s'more.

Anyone who has ever had a s'more can tell you they are not necessarily their favorite sweet. You could try now and ask someone to choose his or her favorite dessert. They would probably make a list of treats and sweets, but s'mores might not make the list. This doesn't mean they don't like s'mores. It just means that there's something about them that doesn't fixate on the taste. There is something more to the s'more than just the flavor. The secret is in its creation.

The creation of s'mores is a group activity. Someone puts out the graham crackers on paper plates. They organize the chocolate bars and put out the sticks upon which one will roast their marshmallows. During the roasting of the marshmallows, there's normally a bit of laughter and critique regarding how someone chooses to roast them. Some choose an even rotisserie—gaining a golden brown that covers the entire marshmallow. Others choose to lightly heat their marshmallow—giving it a barely gooey center and keeping it clean. And a select few will simply thrust their sticks into the fire—setting their marshmallow ablaze.

Laughter is often shared as people try and eat these treats without causing a mess on their faces. Joy is shared as people bask in the warm glow of the fire and have conversations about their lives. The joy of the s'more is not in the treat, but rather, the joy is found in the time shared in the creation of the treat.

Often, we are left thinking that whatever activity we are participating in will only have an opportunity to focus on that activity, but have you ever been to church? If going to church was to *only* go and listen to the pastor preach, then how do we explain the joy that is shared when we are there, serving with our loved ones? Take a moment and think about the activities God has placed on your heart. Don't you think God might have something more than your understanding of what He's called you to do?

LORD, I KNOW THIS LIFE IS AN ADVENTURE. I KNOW THAT WHAT YOU HAVE CALLED ME TO DO GOES DEEPER THAN MY UNDERSTANDING OF IT. REMIND ME THAT THERE IS ALWAYS A BIGGER PICTURE THAN MY PERSPECTIVE, AND THAT PICTURE IS ONE THAT POINTS TO YOU AND YOUR GLORY. AMEN.

59

Daily Vitamins

**"This book of instruction must not depart
from your mouth; you are to meditate on it day
and night so that you may carefully observe
everything written in it. For then you will
prosper and succeed in whatever you do."**

JOSHUA 1:8

Ever since Jerry turned forty, his wife has been insistent on his daily dosage of what seems like dozens of vitamins. When he began taking his different pills and chewables, he immediately looked at the task as somewhat daunting. He hated the notion of starting each and every day with opening various bottles and jars—taking multicolored pills that he'd never seemed to need before. To be honest, Jerry hated it. There are even a few days that this daily morning ritual is seen as a bit of an inconvenience. Still, it is something he takes the time to do every morning.

At first, he viewed the activity as something that would appease his wife. He assumed that by taking his glucosamine pills, his fish oil tablets, and his multi-vitamin chews he would be able to make his wife happy. Something, however, started changing. It was a slow process, but he noticed his joints started creaking a little less. His heart started beating with a stronger, steadier rhythm. Even his muscular aches from daily workouts didn't seem to last as long. He knew that is was not just the vitamins that were contributing to his healthy lifestyle, but they definitely seemed to be helping.

For many of us, we often think that our daily taking of vitamins could be seen through the similar lens of daily reading our Bible. We know we should. We know it is good for our daily walks with the Lord. We know it improves our ability to take up our cross each day. Still, all of us have had moments where we view the reading of Scripture as some form of inconvenience. It seems to be something that holds back our desires to do more of what we want in life. Like Jerry, we may know what's good for us, but still not want to actually do what is good for us.

And yet, we can almost identify those that are in the Bible each and every day. We know them by the way that they act and talk. We can sense the spiritual health in these people in such a way that it's obvious that they are spending time with the Lord. In the same way that we can tell if someone is exercising everyday or are eating healthy the majority of the time, we can identify those that have a deep relationship with the Word of God.

The Bible should be our daily dosage. The Word of God should be something that we take in each and every day with excitement and ease. It should not be something that we simply put on the shelf and take in once every now and again. Like taking one's vitamins, they don't have the same kind of lasting effect if we simply take them once or twice a week. Like the joy that comes from living a healthy lifestyle, the daily reading of the Word is something that cannot be explained.

LORD, I KNOW THERE ARE TIMES THAT I DO NOT JUMP INTO YOUR WORD LIKE I SHOULD. SOMETIMES, I LOOK AT IT AS AN INCONVENIENCE. REMIND ME OF THE JOY THAT COMES FROM DIVING INTO YOUR WORD EVERY MOMENT THAT I CAN. AMEN.

Entry Air-Conditioning

**He renews my life; he leads me along
the right paths for his name's sake.**

PSALM 23:3

When we think about the "big-box" stores, we often think about all of the items that can be bought at these places: office supplies, furniture, groceries, electronics, and various knick-knacks that are sold exclusively within its twenty-foot walls. Something that each and every one of these giant stores has in common is their entrance. They may sell similar products, but there are just enough variations from these stores that set them a part from one another. The one thing, however, that stands out about these stores is the blaring whir and the strong breeze of arctic winds that hit each and every customer that walks past the sliding glass doors.

For some it is sometimes seen as a nuisance. After all, is there really this kind of need for that level of air-conditioning when the weather is rather mild? There, however, is never a complaint when individuals walk into these stores on a hot summer day. When it is reaching triple digits outside and there are heat advisories carrying warnings for people that might be outside in the heat, sometimes the entry-way of these stores is the closest simulation these people can get to a breath of fresh air. There is never a complaint about the frigid air hitting the faces of those who are wiping away sweat. There is a relaxed joy that seems to come over each and every one of the faces of each patron who enter these buildings.

Our Christian lives are not much different when we think about it. Let's face it. We live in a world that is consumed with hardship and dissatisfaction. Spiritually, we often feel as if we are wandering through a desert. People are angry with what is on the news. They are dissatisfied with their relationships or their careers. They may even struggle with the notion of actually finding joy in their church. Because of this, we can almost feel dehydrated and exhausted from having to deal with this level of negativity. So, what do we do? Well, not to sound to obvious, but how often do we consider going to God in prayer?

Like those giant stores, the moment we enter into an intentional time of prayer, we can almost find an immediate sense of peace and joy because we've taken time to escape from the "heat" of the outside world. When the world's drama and frustrations seem to be at a boiling point, instead of jumping head-first into that scolding heat, take time to go to God in prayer and find a joy that eliminates the notion of that heat and allows you to focus on entering an intentional place of prayer.

LORD, SOMETIMES I ALLOW MYSELF TO GET SO CAUGHT UP IN ALL OF THE FRUSTRATIONS OF THE WORLD THAT I FORGET JUST HOW REFRESHING A TIME WITH YOU CAN BE. REMIND ME OF THAT JOY EACH TIME I'M IN PRAYER WITH YOU AND GIVE ME MORE AND MORE OPPORTUNITIES TO SPEND TIME WITH YOU. AMEN.

61

Playground Antics

Everyone should look out not only for his own interests, but also for the interests of others.

PHILIPPIANS 2:4

Cole has always just been a big kid. A little bit of a backstory will tell you that he is the oldest of five kids by quite a bit. We've all known of someone with this story, but Cole's parents had such a difficult time having him they just assumed they would only have one child, but then, years later, they would have a little surprise, then another, and another, and another until, finally, on Cole's sixteenth birthday, they took a family picture showing Cole at sixteen, his brother at eight, his next brother at six, and his twin sisters at four. One would think that Cole had a bit of a problem with this dynamic, but he'll be the first to tell you that after growing up in a quiet house, it's kind of nice to have a little noise.

What stands out about Cole aside from his age is his size. He stands at six feet, seven inches. He's muscular and plays multiple sports. He's definitely what some would call "All-American." He's relatively popular in his school and has plenty of friends his own age, but when he's with his younger siblings, he's not too grown-up to play with them. He still swings with them, plays on jungle gyms with them, and even goes down slides with them. He loves his younger siblings. In fact, that's where he chose to celebrate his sixteenth birthday—at the local playground.

A few eyebrows raised when he chose such a venue until he admitted he just wanted to have a day with his family. That's where they took a family photo that would sit in the living room for all guests to see. You'd see twin girls sitting on their mother's lap. You'd see a father holding an eight-year-old under one arm and a six-year-old under the other, and in the background, you'd find Cole—riding a spring-loaded rocking horse meant for a toddler.

Years later, Cole would be asked about that picture, and he would say with a grin, "I wanted my family to enjoy themselves more than I wanted to have a day that was simply dedicated to me." So many of us allow special days like birthdays to turn ourselves into living idols. We almost expect to be worshiped on these special days. Instead of having the expectation of people bringing joy to you, try making these an occasion to give joy to others. You might just be surprised at the joy that comes back to you.

LORD, I KNOW THERE ARE TIMES WHEN I
ALLOW EXPECTATIONS TO BE THE DEFINITION
OF JOY. ALLOW ME TO BE ABLE TO SPREAD
JOY TO OTHERS AND NOT SIMPLY HAVE THE
EXPECTATION OF JOY BEING GIVEN TO ME. AMEN.

62

Newspaper Routes

Whatever you do, do it from the heart, as something done for the Lord and not for people.

COLOSSIANS 3:23

There are many "first jobs" that are no longer in the same level of existence as they originally were. There were times that before one turned sixteen there were still ample opportunities to make a little bit of money before one could actually get a job at the proper age. You would find thirteen-year-olds working on farms. You might see a few preteens mowing yards for extra cash, but the select few could be entrusted in small towns all across America with a newspaper route.

Kids all over America would show up at a news press, collect as many papers as they could carry, get on their bikes, and toss them on porches, at front doors, in mailboxes, and on driveways throughout various neighborhoods all across town. They would then return to collect more papers or would return to collect their pay for running their route. Because newsprint has, more or less, started to fade from society, so have newspaper routes, which is a shame.

It's a shame for a couple of reasons. For one, preteens lose a way to make more money to save for a car, future dates, or even college, but there is an even greater reason why the disappearance of these job opportunities is such sad news. The fact is that these jobs taught lessons that seem to have almost fallen through the cracks in our society. They showed the importance of being prepared. They taught why it is so important to not allow the day to slip away from you. Newspaper routes, above all else, taught the joy that comes from a hard day's work at a young age.

Many people don't discover that joy until they are well into college. They may have snapshots of that kind of joy in school when they accomplish large projects or are a part of a team that has trained hard, but there is nothing quite like a day of hard work and the enjoyment of the benefits of that work. So, how do we teach those lessons today? How do relive the joy of hard work?

Well, the first thing we can do is look at work as a joy and not a burden. Being able to work holds the very acknowledgment of the gifts and abilities God has given each and every one of us. A long day's work is a joy because it was spent using the gifts God has given you. The same way God blesses children with energy and endurance to ride bikes through town and deliver papers, God has given you special talents to get through the day and take joy in knowing that the day was spent using those talents.

LORD, THANK YOU FOR WORK. I KNOW THAT SOMETIMES I LOOK AT WORK AS IF IT IS SOME KIND OF BURDEN. ALLOW ME TO RECOGNIZE MY GIFTS AND USE THOSE GIFTS EACH DAY IN THE WORK THAT YOU HAVE GIVEN ME. AMEN.

63

A Little Bit of Pain

Dear friends, don't be surprised when the fiery ordeal comes among you to test you as if something unusual were happening to you. Instead, rejoice as you share in the sufferings of Christ, so that you may also rejoice with great joy when his glory is revealed.

1 PETER 4:12–13

That sounds like a rather strange title to find in a book about joy. It goes without saying that pain is rarely the holder of joy, but ask any exercise enthusiast and they will tell you quite the opposite. If you were to walk into the nearest gym with weight-lifting equipment or cardio machines, you'll rarely find anyone with a pleasant look on their face during the activity. And yet, these places are normally crowded with people who are waiting for opportunities to use these pieces of fitness equipment.

Some spend hours upon hours in these facilities lifting heavy weights, running long distances, and yet not moving from a physical spot. As they are performing all of these physical feats, they start to sweat, their bodies fatigue, and they start giving off a less than pleasant odor. From the outside looking in, it almost seems like these people are putting their bodies through various amounts of torture, and still, the fitness industry is a multi-billion dollar business. They are literally making money off of the sweat of the consumer's brow.

Still, people participate in the building of one's own body. Even at the cost of their own comfort, they find great joy in the uncomfortable. Why is this? What is it about these activities that have captured our culture as a whole? We can't watch movies without an actor showing off their physical prowess. We can't be on social media without finding someone's fitness journey. We can't even listen to music without finding playlists that are dedicated to one's need for a workout. The fact is, there are some things in life that give a little discomfort *and* a lot of joy.

Why is this? What is it about these activities that give a little discomfort that we still pursue? What makes them so special? Well, as with exercise, there are moments in life that cause a little bit of pain but bring about a great deal of joy. That treadmill might be exhausting every time one sets foot on it, but running that marathon is something that yields joy and pride in one's accomplishments. That early morning workout might be difficult, but not as difficult as living an obese lifestyle.

Spiritually, it might be an inconvenience to set aside time to pray or read the Bible, but have you ever heard of someone who said their time in the Word was not worth the time that was spent? Have you ever known someone to spend time in prayer and come out thinking it was just a waste of time? Of course, not! Even though we have all been guilty of looking at the giving up of our time as an inconvenience, there is nothing quite like the joy that is found in the overcoming of that attitude and spending it with God.

LORD, I KNOW SOMETIMES I ACT LIKE IT IS PAINFUL TO GIVE UP MY TIME TO SPEND IT WITH YOU. ALLOW ME TO REALIZE THERE IS A JOY ON THE OTHER SIDE OF MY INCONVENIENCE THAT IS WORTH SACRIFICE OF GIVING UP THAT TIME. AMEN.

64

From Scratch

**"The people I formed for myself
will declare my praise."**

ISAIAH 43:21

With all of the cooking shows and all of the recipes that are shared on social media, it's no surprise that we've seen quite an uptick in our culture for the desire to learn how to cook. Individuals are doing their best to close the microwave for good and pick up pots, pans, and spatulas. They are leaving the drive-thru window and keeping their eyes on the window of an oven. For better or worse, we are becoming a culture that has rediscovered a love for cooking.

Some cultures within our country, however, have not seemed to lose their joy of cooking. For some, it is simply what they do. It is the family tradition to make something from scratch. Some of us are just now discovering that "from scratch" means more than simply opening a box and putting the ingredients together. It means actual creation.

This is something that has baffled a great deal of young cooks and bakers, but the "from scratch" concept is something that is changing the world of baking. There has been a return to the old ways of baking. Even down to the simplest of creations: bread. For many of us, bread is something that has its own section in the grocery store. Bread is not necessarily something we create.

It is something that we buy, and yet, bread making is one of the old art forms that seems to be making a bit of a comeback.

There is one family who takes the "from scratch" method seriously. For instance, instead of flour, they purchase their own grain and make their own flour. They say it is what makes their bread recipes special. The older ones in the family will even claim there is something different about each batch because they've taken the time to create it from the barest of ingredients. They have even made it part of the Christmas gift to families in the church by making their famous Cinnamon Wheat Bread and giving it out at the Christmas service.

Many of us forget the joy in knowing that we all came from very little. Scientifically, we understand that we grew in our mother's womb from a bundle of cells and into the humans we are today, but those of us who know God take joy in knowing there was so much more than just that. There was our Father, intricately knitting us together, making us who we are today. How can there be no greater joy than knowing God made us . . . from scratch.

LORD, THANK YOU FOR CREATING ME. THANK YOU FOR KNITTING ME TOGETHER AND MAKING ME INTO THE PERSON I AM TODAY. ALLOW ME TO HAVE THIS SAME KIND OF APPRECIATION FOR OTHERS—FOR JUST AS YOU HAVE MADE ME, YOU ALSO MADE THEM. AMEN.

65

Personality Profiles

But you are a chosen race, a royal priesthood, a holy nation, a people for his possession, so that you may proclaim the praises of the one who called you out of darkness into his marvelous light.

1 PETER 2:9

We've all seen them. Most of us have taken them. The fact is that we are a people who have become a little obsessed with personality tests. We have come to know the joy of knowing the type of person we are. For some of us, it even goes as deep as the placement of one's identity. It may not be something we're proud of, but all of us have seen the quizzes and wondered which character from our beloved television show or movie we would be like. We wonder which color defines us, or what kind of animal we would be. Some of these assessments have become so popular that they have even been implemented in the workplace. Assessments like the Enneagram, the Meyers-Briggs, and even StrengthFinders have been used to identify the way a person works, thinks, and cooperates with other members of a team. All of this to answer a simple question, "Where do we belong?"

It's a question mankind has pondered for thousands of years. It's a notion that has bounced about the minds of our greatest thinkers, and has occupied the musings of children. We want to know who we are, whom we belong to, and what makes us special and unique. These are emotions that all of us have felt to some degree. Whether we like to admit it or not, we want to know how the world sees us. We like the idea of finding our place in society. All of this, however, is superficial.

Who we are, where we belong, and what it all means are answered with the reality of who God is in our lives. For me, I've always thought of God looking at us through a synonymous lens as that of a parent. Those who have children understand there is a depth that goes far deeper than one can really describe when it comes down to the identity of their child. The love one has for their children should be one that is difficult to describe at the very least. And in that, we find the point. Our identity may be something we fixate on, but there is a God who knows who we are at a deeper level than our own understanding. We are His creation. He knows our hearts and our minds on a more meaningful level. There is a joy in knowing we are loved by a God who knows our identity better than we could ever describe ourselves. It's one of the many reasons we find joy in noting that the first part of our identity is a child of God—being able to understand love without being able to describe it.

FATHER, THANK YOU FOR LOVING ME. I KNOW THERE ARE TIMES THAT I GET SO CAUGHT UP IN THE NOTION OF FINDING OUT WHO I AM AS A PERSON THAT I FORGET TO ADMIT I AM YOURS AT THE END OF THE DAY. REMIND ME OF YOUR LOVE EACH DAY AND REMIND ME THAT THIS LOVE HAS A DEPTH THAT CAN'T BE DESCRIBED. AMEN.

66

The Block Tower

**He has made everything appropriate in
its time. He has also put eternity in their
hearts, but no one can discover the work
God has done from beginning to end.**

ECCLESIASTES 3:11

There is a stack of blocks in an office workspace that has become quite the office challenge among the nine or ten contenders who have chosen to participate. There are about seven or eight onlookers who have enjoyed the show enough without participating, even though they are always welcome to join in on the competition. The premise is simple: the tower is built with rectangular blocks. A player can pull a block from the tower and use that block to build on to the top of the tower. When the game starts, the tower is right at eight inches tall. As the players continue to participate throughout the day, as they are walking through the office, the tower gets a little bit taller and a little unstable. Right now the office record is one foot and three inches. Many attempts have come close, but it is still the winning height for a little more than four months now.

What's interesting about this little competition is that there really is no technical winner. In most competitions, there is the desire for a clear winner and a clear loser. This is not the case for this game. The idea of the game is to simply keep it going. Ideally, the game never ends. The tower climbs and climbs, and even though it would be incredibly unstable, the game would continue past the ceiling tiles, through the roof, and into the clouds.

There's a lesson to be learned from this little block tower. So many of us look to be the winner of something. We look to find an end to a means. We want the promotion more than we want to work in our jobs. We want our kids to get straight A's but don't take time to work with them in their education. We want to have the nice yard, but forget it takes constant care in order to have the "yard of the month" reward. We even talk about getting in shape as if it's a temporary battle against our self-control, when every fitness enthusiast will tell you that health is a lifestyle, nothing more, nothing less.

When we take the time to realize the kind of joy that comes from not looking for a destination and rather focusing on the journey, we are able to live a more fulfilled life. Sometimes in life, there is not an end to a journey. Sometimes, things were meant to last beyond a specific time frame. Like our relationship with God, the joy that comes from knowing Him is one that is being constantly built. There is no cap when it comes down to knowing God. Seek Him out and discover the joy that comes from knowing Him.

LORD, I HAVE FOCUSED ON FINDING AN END TO MANY THINGS IN MY LIFE. REMIND ME THAT THERE IS NO END WHEN IT COMES DOWN TO KNOWING YOU. REMIND ME THAT I WILL NEVER FULLY KNOW YOU AND I CAN ONLY GROW DEEPER IN KNOWING YOU AS I SEEK YOU OUT EACH DAY. AMEN.

67

Paperclip Chains

**Now if by grace, then it is not by works;
otherwise grace ceases to be grace.**

ROMANS 11:6

Miss Combs does something rather unique for her first graders. In elementary education, she spends all day with her students. She keeps up with twenty-two students throughout the entire school year. She learns names, meets parents, and plans curriculum for every subject from science to spelling. She is good at her job as far as her role in content is concerned, but that is not why the parents have come to love her role in their children's lives. You see, Miss Combs is known that the "paperclip teacher." That is how she is introduced at school functions and how her students describe her to parents.

This designation started a few years ago when Miss Combs decided to participate in a yearlong experiment. The experiment would comprise of buying tiny paperclips and making a chain for her students at the beginning of each year. The experiment was simple. For every good thing that a student did, she would add a paperclip to the chain. For every bad thing a student did, she would remove a paperclip from the chain. She kept a tally each day for everything the students did, whether they realized it or not. If they said "Yes, ma'am," they got a paperclip. If they played nicely, they got a paperclip. If they shared some of their snacks, they got a paperclip. She would never tell the students whether they received a paperclip or not. She would keep the tallies to herself and add or erase them throughout the day, and at the end of her day as she was getting ready to leave, she would add onto the chains.

The beauty of this was that every student, no matter how disruptive or disrespectful, always seemed to get one or two each day. At the end of the year, parents would be able to see the length of the paperclip chains of their students and keep track of the kind of impact their child had on their teacher. No matter what, however, every child had at least one paperclip for each of the nearly two hundred days that the students spent at school.

One parent, who was a little more honest than others, wondered how their child had a chain that was nearly three hundred paperclips in length. Miss Combs' response was one that I think all of us should take into account. She gave her trademark smile and said, "The actual experiment calls for two chains; one representing the good, and the other representing bad. For me, the good doesn't necessarily represent their actions so much as it represents who they are to me. Even though all students do bad things, it does not change the fact that there is something about each and every one of them that deserves to be loved. The chain represents when they've shown that kind of love to others." In life, we focus so much on our actions or works in order to gain favor from God, but that's not how we were called to live. God loves us even when we do bad and regardless of whether or not we do good.

LORD, I KNOW I GET SO WRAPPED UP IN DOING THE RIGHT THING IN ORDER TO EARN YOUR LOVE. REMIND ME EACH DAY THAT YOUR LOVE IS NOT EARNED, BUT INSTEAD IS SOMETHING THAT HAS BEEN GIVEN TO US. AMEN.

68

Striking Features

"In the same way, let your light shine before others, so that they may see your good works and give glory to your Father in heaven."

MATTHEW 5:16

As a young boy, Matthew was told his eyes were going to get him in a lot of trouble. It was a compliment, of course, but it was something he had always been a little self-conscious about. Even his own wife admitted that there was something about his eyes that made him stand out. His eyes were gray, but there was such brilliance to them that many thought they were silver. Men were struck and women swooned just about every time he made eye contact with them. Because of this, Matthew had become a bit of an introvert over the years.

Into his adulthood, Matthew developed a bit of a subconscious fear about his eyes, worrying that the only reason anyone would have any interest in him was because of his striking features. After years of living with this assumption, he had finally had enough and came to his wife—explaining the insecurity about his eyes. He even went as far as to wonder whether or not they would have ever married if not for those eyes. His wife lovingly laughed at his self-deprecation. She asked him where they met. He responded that they met at camp.

"What were you doing when we met?" she asked.

"I was playing with my younger brother," he said.

"I fell in love with you because I saw how tender and loving you were with others. I watched you for a few days after that from a distance. We were too far apart for me to really get a good look at those eyes of yours. What I love about you is how you love others. You could have unnoticeable brown eyes and I would have still been struck in the way that you love."

Many times, we wonder about what God has done in us that makes us special. We never really take the time to assume that the special thing about us is not necessarily what can be seen as a physical characteristic. More often than not, what makes us striking is found in how we interact with others. God has made each and every one of us striking in our own special way—and to be completely frank, what makes us truly striking rarely has anything to do with the way we look, but rather in the way that we love. God did not create us so superficially that we could only be known by our appearance. God made us to love Him and love others around us. How we do that is what gives us the kind of striking features that point to God and His glory.

LORD, I KNOW YOU HAVE TAKEN TIME TO MAKE ME UNIQUELY. I TAKE JOY IN KNOWING THAT WHAT MAKES ME SPECIAL IS NOT ONLY HOW YOU HAVE MADE ME LOOK, BUT MORE SO ON HOW YOU HAVE CALLED ME TO LOVE. AMEN.

69

"I'll Be Just a Minute . . ."

. . . so also Christ, having been offered once to bear the sins of many, will appear a second time, not to bear sin, but to bring salvation to those who are waiting for him.

HEBREWS 9:28

Ask any ten-year-old and they will tell you that this phrase is one of the biggest lies ever told. "I'll just be a minute . . ." is one of those phrases that all of us use to communicate one thing and one thing only. We are saying, "I don't know when I'll be back, but just know I'm working hard for that moment." At least, that is what most children hear when they are told this.

Think about when this line was thrown about when you were a child. There was always a tinge of frustration over not knowing the exact moment of one's return, but there was never a question on whether or not they would return. Even when we were not sure how long they would be gone, we always knew, deep down, that Mom or Dad was going to return. Think about it. If there was ever a time that we questioned whether or not our loved one's would return, it would be a time filled with apprehension and constant devastation every time they left to do anything.

It reminds me of Christ speaking of when He would return. There was no mention of the exact date. There was no conversation on the hour of the day. The disciples were simply left with the promise of a return. To be fair, many of us live in a world that has forgotten that Christ will one day return. One day we will all be faced with the joy of seeing Christ again. The only frustrating thing about this reality is that so many of us live as if the reality is nothing more than myth or a possibility. Many of us forget to live like Christ could return at any moment.

This does not mean we have to live a life of near perfection, nor do we have to keep up appearances. It means actually living with the kind of joy in knowing there will come a time when we are face-to-face with the one who has given us a sense of perfect love. How could we hold on to anger or legalistic attitudes when we know that Christ could return? It is not like a parent returning to discipline us for every wrong thing we have ever done. It is a reunion with the God that gave His Son for us and has promised to return. He'll be just a minute . . .

LORD, JESUS, I KNOW THERE WILL COME
A TIME WHEN YOU RETURN. ALLOW ME TO
LIVE A LIFE KNOWING THAT THIS DAY IS
FAST APPROACHING AND INSTEAD OF FEAR,
REMIND ME TO LIVE IN JOY. AMEN.

70

Puzzle Competitions

**For every activity there is a right time and procedure,
even though a person's troubles are heavy on him.**

ECCLESIASTES 8:6

Not many people have the special kind of patience that is required to put a puzzle together. We all can handle the typical one-hundred-piece puzzle without much fuss, but there are a few puzzles that get into the thousands. Many families have at least one puzzle in their home. Some have multiple boxes. Some choose a scene from nature to piece together, whereas some might choose to piece together a famous work of art. Whatever the case may be, it takes patience and perseverance in order to finish a puzzle. Something interesting that has started to occur across the country is the implementation of puzzle competitions. Teams gather—all putting together the same puzzle in hopes they can finish their puzzle first.

That's an interesting notion because these competitions seem to take the whole point of putting puzzles together and then destroying it. How can anyone expect to have a sense of patience when someone is timed? Isn't the point of a puzzle to be something that is calming? Even though this does not seem the case, that is the number one strategy to winning a puzzle completion; stay calm and be patient. Those that frantically piece together the puzzle end up getting flustered when the piece they are searching for does not appear when they want it to appear.

Any seasoned puzzler will be the first to tell you that the best way to win is to simply relax and acknowledge that the piece will appear when it's ready to appear. Instead of worrying about one specific piece to fill your perspective of the puzzle, focus on the bigger picture and help those on your team to fill out their parts of the puzzle.

When we get down to the heart of the matter, life can seem like one big puzzle that we are racing to finish. We want to know how our days will go and often get flustered when our plans have gone awry. How do we handle these frustrations? More often than not, we frantically search for the plan to make everything work out as we assume it should. There is no room for joy in this mind-set. Don't get caught up in making sure that every single detail needs to work out the way you want. Instead, have faith in knowing that we serve a God that knows the whole puzzle and knows when and where each piece will fall into place.

LORD, I ADMIT THAT I OFTEN FIXATE ON MAKING SURE THERE IS A PLAN. ALLOW ME TO LET GO OF THE NOTION THAT EVERY SINGLE DETAIL NEEDS TO FALL INTO PLACE. REMIND ME THAT YOU ARE GOD, THERE IS A PLAN, AND I DON'T HAVE TO KNOW EVERY PIECE OF THE PUZZLE. AMEN.

The Mission Trip

**. . . in all your ways know him, and he
will make your paths straight.**

PROVERBS 3:6

Julie is what you would call a perfectionist when it comes down to planning. There is no room for error in her plan. She does not like loose ends, and she despises being told, "Everything will be okay." When she makes a plan, she sticks to it. She does not deviate from the plan. As a mission's director, she has come to realize the importance of planning. Something she has come to admit about herself, however, is that she is not a fan of a plan with a lot of moving parts. She has even coined a phrase in staff meetings, "The more parts in a machine, the more you will inevitably have to fix." Because of this mentality, she has stayed in a relative comfort zone of her ministry.

Her comfort zone is the Americas. She is perfectly fine with going anywhere on this side of the prime meridian. She has served in the upper parts of Canada as well as the southern parts of Argentina. She has developed contacts all over the western hemisphere over the years of traveling to these places. Because of this, her planning is fairly relaxed. She calls up pastors. She makes itineraries, sets up payment plans, buys tickets, and then she goes. Normally, her mission trips run very smoothly. This upcoming one, however, is not the case.

During her last mission trip, she was invited to lead her first mission trip in Africa. Even though she had been to Africa, she had never set foot on the continent in a leadership role. That frustrated her to no end. She had never planned a trip in this part of the world. She had no contacts. She had no cultural context to be able to understand the happenings of each day. For her, it was going to be a nightmare putting this plan together, and worse than that, her son had the audacity to say, "Everything will be okay." Just as she was about to give him a piece of her mind, her son asked with an innocent smile, "Would God allow us to go on mission there if we weren't supposed to be there?"

As flustered as she was at the statement, she had to acknowledge the level of truth in his words. For many of us, when something is outside of our comfort zone, we immediately assume that it is to be classified as not good. This is not always the case. We were not called to be comfortable. Christianity has never been something that has promised the country club lifestyle, but there is the promise of joy at the end of hardship. Years later, Julie would be going on her fifth trip to Africa. Her son was serving there full-time and she could not be happier for what God did with her family during that first uncomfortable trip to Africa.

FATHER, I KNOW I WILL OFTEN AVOID THE SITUATIONS THAT ARE GOING TO BE A LITTLE UNCOMFORTABLE. I KNOW THESE MOMENTS WILL COME IN MY LIFE. ALLOW ME TO MOVE FORWARD THROUGH THESE MOMENTS AND RECOGNIZE THE JOY THAT COMES FROM THEM. AMEN.

72

The Light Section

**For this is what the Lord has commanded us:
I have made you a light for the Gentiles to
bring salvation to the end of the earth.**

ACTS 13:47

A bit of a phenomenon occurs, as we get older. There are certain stores that lose their luster as we get older, and other stores that seem to pique our interests when we couldn't stand going in them when we were young. For boys, they often move away from trivial toy stores and move onto the world of gadgets, sports equipment, or hardware stores. No matter how old they get, boys never seem to lose their love of toys. They just grow with them. For girls, they move away from clothing trends that last as long as they're on the rack and move on to an appearance that is either classic or more fitting to their personality. But something has seemed to capture the attention of both sexes is the move toward giant home improvement stores. After all, they have all the toys a boy could want and offer an opportunity to express a sense of style that appeals to female shoppers.

Something that both shoppers have come to enjoy is the light section. No matter the age, it is the one section of the store that catches the eye of most shoppers. The obvious reason for this is because of the fact that it can't go unnoticed. Like moths, many of us find ourselves drifting toward the section in the store to witness the different variations of lights that are offered. Some are meant for dim situations—only allowing enough light to fill the room that won't bother the eyes of those who have adjusted to the darkness of early morning and late night. Others are meant to shine with such brilliance they fill rooms with such light that it almost feels synonymous with the sun.

Whatever the occasion needed for the specific quality of light is not the point. The point is the reality of being drawn to light. All of us have some kind of special desire to seek out light to any degree. When light is available, there is automatically a sense of peace and joy in the recognition of darkness not having a hold on our sense.

Each and every one of us that know Christ has a light to share. It is something so many can recognize. Think of those whom you don't have to wonder whether or not they know Christ. How is that we know without even asking them? Could it be there is some supernatural sense in recognizing the light of those that let it shine? There is a joy in finding light, but there is one even greater when we share it with others. The Bible is clear when it says to not hide one's light. It is not just a commandment, but an encouragement in knowing the kind of joy that comes from letting it shine.

LORD, REMIND ME EACH DAY TO SHARE THE LIGHT YOU HAVE GIVEN ME WITH OTHERS. I KNOW THERE ARE TIMES THAT I ALLOW MYSELF TO PUT MY LIGHT AWAY. KEEP ME AWAY FROM THIS MENTALITY. REMIND ME OF THE JOY THAT COMES FROM SEEING THE LIGHT OF OTHERS, AND REMIND ME OF THE JOY THAT COMES FROM LETTING MY LIGHT SHINE. AMEN.

73

Tears of Joy

**The people here were of more noble character
than those in Thessalonica, since they received
the word with eagerness and examined the
Scriptures daily to see if these things were so.**

ACTS 17:11

Most men will admit they don't exactly know what to do when they are in the presence of a crying woman; mostly because they assume they have done something wrong. Even though that is not always the case, most women will acknowledge there is the possibility that they have either handled a situation incorrectly or have forgotten something of major significance. Every now and again, however, there will come a time when they do something so right that it causes women to cry. This is quite the conundrum for men if it's something they've done inadvertently.

Most men can think of something they've done that has caused tears to form in a woman's eyes in a good way. Maybe they reached a new level of romance in the form of a proposal. Maybe they found a gift they had been wanting for months but assumed they could not get. Maybe they said something touching in a wedding vow. All of these, however, took great amounts of effort, but ask any husband, and he can probably remember a time that he did something so wonderful without thinking that he had to question whether or not he had made a mistake.

Wives often say that it's the little things that matter. There is a great truth in this. Yes, we all enjoy grand gestures from time to time, but those often show that the thought and love behind it was intentional and sometimes, unnatural. Wives talk about the level of joy they have felt when they see their husbands playing with the children instead of lounging on the couch. They point out the swelling of one's heart when they find an unexpected thoughtful note. Sometimes it's just enough to bring tears to their eyes when they come home and realize that all of the chores have been done, dinner has been cooked, or kids are already doing homework. This reveals that joy is not always about the huge gestures of love. Most of the time, it is just carried out by being thoughtful. Joy from the Lord is the same.

It's not always about taking off work to go on the mission trip, nor is it about giving vast amounts of wealth to the church. These are both wonderful things, but you can find the same kind of joy from reading your Bible everyday, from spending daily time with God in prayer, or from having regular fellowship with other Christians. We'll often find joy is not something that is only discovered through the big moments; it is also found in the daily moments where we choose that joy.

LORD, I KNOW THERE ARE TIMES THAT I GET SO FOCUSED ON FINDING JOY IN THE BIG MOMENTS. I HAVE BEEN GUILTY OF FEELING THAT I CAN ONLY FIND JOY IN THOSE BIG MOMENTS. REMIND ME THAT JOY IS A DAILY CHOICE, AND THAT DAILY CHOICE IS YOU. AMEN.

74

Bad Haircuts

He also said to them: "Suppose one of you has a friend and goes to him at midnight and says to him, 'Friend, lend me three loaves of bread, because a friend of mine on a journey has come to me, and I don't have anything to offer him.' Then he will answer from inside and say, 'Don't bother me! The door is already locked, and my children and I have gone to bed. I can't get up to give you anything.' I tell you, even though he won't get up and give him anything because he is his friend, yet because of his friend's shameless boldness, he will get up and give him as much as he needs."

LUKE 11:5–8

Keith has a bit of a curse. He seems to always have a bad hair day. In fact, it has become his trademark to some degree. People can often tell if a person is him or not simply by observing the cropped follicles sprouting from his skull. Because he never seems to make a fuss over it, the topic of his hair never seems to come up in conversation. People just assume that he's one of those gentlemen that either does not care about his hair's appearance or has given up a long time ago. What's interesting is many people who have known him for a long time actually say it used to be a lot worse. Finally, as a way to inconspicuously find out the source of his hairstyle, a coworker asked where he got his haircut.

Keith grinned, and without missing a beat he asked, "Is it that bad?" As his friends tried to reassure him his hair wasn't that bad, he finally waved their vain attempts to make him feel better away and said, "My wife cuts my hair . . ."

There was a silence that fell over the group. They did not know how to respond to the statement. How could they politely tell their friend that his wife did not know how to cut hair? Keith could see the tenseness that was spreading throughout the table and let out a laugh. When it did not ease the confusion among his group of friends and coworkers, he finally said, "My wife is working on a beautician license. When we had kids, she had to put her goals on hold to take care of the children, and I had to pick up a few extra shifts at work. We could not afford to get her books or videos to teach her some of the finer points. So, she needed a practice dummy. I'm the practice dummy."

Many times, we forget about something I'd like to call the joy of inconvenience. So many times, when we serve others, we try to do it on our own terms. We try and make it fit in a way where whatever we're doing serves us just as much as we are serving. We don't often realize that service sometimes comes with a sense of inconvenience. It might cost us our time, our money, and for people like Keith, even our hair! Does this mean the service is not worth it? Does it mean there is not joy to be found when we sacrifice for the betterment of others? Keith, for the sake of his wife, happily says this about his hair, "It's easy to sacrifice a little bit of hair for the woman that I love a lot."

LORD, I OFTEN FORGET THERE IS A JOY THAT'S FOUND IN THE MOMENTS THAT I SERVE. THE REASON IS BECAUSE I FOCUS ON THE THINGS I'LL LOSE. ALLOW ME TO FOCUS ON THE ONES I'M SERVING INSTEAD OF FOCUSING ON THE SACRIFICE I'VE MADE IN THE SERVICE. AMEN.

75

"I Should Probably . . ."

The integrity of the upright guides them, but the perversity of the treacherous destroys them.

PROVERBS 11:3

We've all said it. It may not have been over the exact same thing, nor has it always been said at the exact time, but we've all started a sentence with "I should probably . . ." Sometimes it could be said in regards to our health. Sometimes, it might be said about our career. Sometimes, it could even be used to describe our own relationships. Whatever the case may be, the little phrase, "I should probably . . ." is the recognition of something vital to all of our lives.

At this point there is probably some level of pondering over what exactly this has to do with joy. After all, admitting we should probably do anything is almost the admittance of foregoing joy. I don't necessarily believe this is the case. Let's think about our health, for instance. When we say we should probably start exercising or we should probably start eating better foods, we are not saying we are not claiming a joy over our current health. If that were the case, why would there ever be a need for change if we were happy with the way we looked or felt? When we talk about how we should probably get to work, we are acknowledging that there would be some level of joy that was missed because we didn't take the time to work for those that need us to provide for them. And when we admit we should probably go home to spend time with our families, we are acknowledging that there is a joy that will be missed if we do not return to the our loved ones.

The point of "I should probably . . ." is not a relinquishing of joy. It's quite the opposite. It's the taking hold of joy. It's the leaving of one's current circumstances and moving to a place of true joy. When we say, "I should probably . . ." we are not saying that our life is the way we want it, but we have to go and give that up for some kind of greater good. That whole notion doesn't even make sense. If it is for the greater good, then why would we not take that step with joy? So go to the gym, eat healthy, work hard, provide for your family, spend time with the kids, love your spouse. Don't do it because you *probably should*. Do it for joy.

LORD, I KNOW I HAVE DONE SO MANY THINGS WITH AN "I SHOULD PROBABLY . . ." ATTITUDE. I KNOW I HAVE BEEN GUILTY OF THIS MIND-SET. ALLOW ME TO RECOGNIZE THE JOY IN CHASING AFTER THE GOOD. AMEN.

76

Classically Trained

**But you are to proclaim things
consistent with sound teaching.**

TITUS 2:1

Ome of the most prominent things one can say in the musical community is whether or not one has had classical training. Many musicians these days can definitely claim a steady level of expertise in their music, but a vast majority cannot claim the experience of learning music in the classical sense. Many musicians learn through the school of trial and error—testing different sounds at such a repetitive rate they simply learn the notes by ear. Some may not ever learn the technical vernacular associated with the musical world but can play with every bit of skill that a classically trained musician may possess. So why is classical training such a sought-after quality in musicians? Why is it so important for someone to have the proper training required for many musicians? If a musician whose learning has come from the one's ear can play the same music, why should it make a difference?

Well, the fact of the matter is, there is a certain level of communication in the discussion of one's training. It says that instead of placing sounds together and discovering which sounds blend and work together in the best ways, it communicates there was a deeper learning that took place that allows a musician to understand music without even having to play it in the first place. They can take a sheet of notes and place them in their mind, being able to get a strong idea of how the music should sound before they even start playing the instrument or singing the song.

There's a joy that comes from the kind of assurance in knowing that you know what you are talking about. The Bible is similar in this instance. For many of us, we sometime settle for the slapping together of various verses from the Bible and pretend those are enough to communicate some kind of deeper knowledge of the Bible. They allow these verses to take precedence over the actual reading of Scripture. When one settles for this type of learning of Scripture, they miss out on a deeper, richer understanding of what the Word of God actually says. We learn that Philippians 4:13 is not talking about achieving the impossible so much as it is the encouraging words of a man in prison. We learn that the Old Testament is not just a container of stories *before* Christ, we realize that the Old Testament is a collection of words that all point *to* Christ.

Don't settle for the simple memorization of verses from your Bible study. Memorization is a practice that is all well and good, but there's so much more to the Bible than just the cherry-picking of verses and using those to apply to our daily lives. Take time to actually study the Word; there's a joy that goes farther than the simple reading of one or two verses.

LORD, I ADMIT THERE ARE TIMES THAT I HAVE SETTLED FOR SIMPLY LOOKING AT A VERSE OR TWO AND ACCEPTING THAT AS A TIME OF BIBLICAL STUDY. REMIND ME OF THE RICHNESS OF YOUR WORD. ALLOW ME TO ALWAYS FIND TIME TO SPEND TIME IN YOUR WORD. AMEN.

77

"Mornin' Brother"

He replied to them, "Who are my mother and my brothers?" Looking at those sitting in a circle around him, he said, "Here are my mother and my brothers! Whoever does the will of God is my brother and sister and mother."

MARK 3:33–35

As a teenager, Chris did not know what to think of the church life. It was something that was so bizarre to him. After all, why would anyone in their right mind give up any time on the weekend to gather in a building and hear about a guy that lived two thousand years ago? It just didn't make any sense to him. Being raised in the South, Chris definitely held a cultural understanding of who Jesus was. He was supposedly the Son of God. He lived a perfect life and died on a cross for our sins, whatever that means. Because these were phrases and words that he had heard most of his life from people that invited him to church and his Christian friends, the words had lost their meaning. He could remember a time when they meant something more. He could remember a time when those kinds of words held a sense of mystery, but like all things with time, he had lost interest.

Something he could never understand, however, was the familial tie to the church. Complete strangers would always greet him the same way every single time he entered the church building. He would always get a "Mornin' Brother" from people that had come to know a little bit about him since his first visit. He knew there was no relation between the people who were greeting him, but there was still something special about the way the people cared for one another.

Finally, after months of attending, he went to the pastor after church and finally asked, "Why does everyone here call each other brother or sister?" The pastor's response is something that Chris still quotes to this day. "Those who know Christ are a part of a family who goes beyond the household. I know you don't know Christ, but know that when you're here, you'll always be treated like family."

For many of us, we forget about the joy of going to church with our church family. We seem to think that church is only about worshiping the Lord. While that is a primary objective, one of the tremendous pluses is being able to be part of a family. No matter who you are, where you come from, or what you do, there is always the joy of knowing you're with family, because you're a part of Christ's family.

LORD, THANK YOU FOR MY CHURCH FAMILY.
THANK YOU FOR PUTTING PEOPLE IN MY LIFE
THAT I CAN KNOW DEEPER THAN A FRIENDSHIP
OR AS FELLOW CHURCH ATTENDEES. I
CAN KNOW THEM AS FAMILY. AMEN.

78

The Echo

"For God loved the world in this way: He gave his one and only Son, so that everyone who believes in him will not perish but have eternal life."

JOHN 3:16

Every year, the pastor of a small church in a rural community invites a traveling pastor to participate in a church revival. For those of you who may not remember what those are, church revivals used to be a very common practice. The tactics may differ from pastor to pastor, but essentially, a church would open their doors every single night of the week and there would be a message delivered to the church. Now, with social media, extra-curricular activities, or picking up extra shifts at work, it seems like that kind of church gathering would be an impossibility. Still, the message is relatively the same no matter what church you may find yourself in. The message is that you are loved. God loved you so much that He sent His only Son to die for you and your sins. He conquered death, and the chains of sin no longer hold us down.

As nice as that sentiment is, if you're reading this, you probably already know all of this. So, why even bring it up? Well, as much as we hate to admit it, we can sometimes forget this reality. Obviously, we *know* all about John 3:16. It's not something we have necessarily forgotten, but the reality is sometimes we do need that gentle reminder. We all know that God loves us. That is a given, but sometimes we just forget how much. We forget about the magnitude of the message behind John 3:16. We forget that God as a Father gave His only Son for our sins. He did not do it because we are these ridiculously lovable creatures. God gave us His Son because of the fact that He is the very definition of love.

When we take into account the depth of a love such as that, how can we respond with anything less than joy and adoration? Every year when the pastor leaves to speak at a revival, there is a conversation on why the church chose to have a service every single night. One pastor has given probably the best answer so far. According to him, "Some people are nails. How many times has a nail been slammed into the wood on the first swing of the hammer? As much as we hate to admit it, some people just need the steady repetitive tapping for the message of the gospel to sink in."

LORD, THANK YOU FOR SENDING YOUR SON TO DIE FOR MY SINS. SOMETIMES I FORGET ABOUT THE MESSAGES THAT I LEARNED AS A CHILD. CONSTANTLY REMIND ME OF YOUR GOODNESS, LORD, AND ALLOW ME TO ALWAYS FIND TIME TO BE REMINDED OF THE FACT THAT YOU SENT YOUR SON TO DIE FOR ME. AMEN.

79

Local Weather

**"I have told you these things so that in me you may
have peace. You will have suffering in this world.
Be courageous! I have conquered the world."**

JOHN 16:33

Every household seems to have the sound of some form of media going on in the background of the daily life of the home. For some homes, it is the sound of songs playing from various music apps that fills the background noise. For others, they might have the news carrying the base noise level—informing those of all the catastrophes that are happening in the world. Some, however, keep the local weather playing. They enjoy the soft music that carries the weather updates every ten minutes. People typically feel better about storms when they can see them coming and have plenty of time to prepare for them.

For one elderly couple, they have come to love the meteorologist on the local news channel. They tune into the news to catch up on what is happening in their area, but they will be quick to tell you how much they love the weather-man. It does not matter if the weather is good or bad, rain or shine, sunny or stormy, the weatherman always gives the news in such a way that it feels almost personal. "He treats us like family . . . ," the seventy-five-year-old woman will often remark.

What they especially love about this individual is how he handles the upcoming storms. Living in the Southeast, the family is not exactly intimidated by strong winds, but every now and again, a storm will have just the right conditions to give the family a little bit of unease. The cold winds will blend with the warm conditions of the summer months, and tornadoes will inevitably be predicted. Many in the area will chalk up these kinds of storms as simply just being a part of living in the area, but there are still some that find it a little tumultuous to have to deal with them.

This is where the local weatherman becomes so important to these families. He keeps the families informed on every little thing that is happening with the storm and tells them when to take special precaution. He jumps back and forth from the map to footage of what is going on outside so that the people can get as clear a picture as to what all is happening. As a meteorologist, he does his job proficiently. He is very good at his job, but this is not what makes him special. What makes him such an important figure to so many households is his attitude during the storms. No matter how bad things get, or how strong the winds and rain may become, the weatherman always makes sure they know the storm is only temporary. No matter how bad it gets, it will pass.

So many of us forget this reality. We allow ourselves to think that the bad is here to stay. Because of this, we allow so much negativity to take a permanent residence in our hearts. Even after the situation has passed, we often fixate on the negativity that was born from it. This is not how we were called to live. There is no joy in this kind of lifestyle. Let go of the frustration and know that each and every storm, no matter how terrible, will always come to pass.

LORD, THANK YOU FOR BEING WITH ME DURING THE DARK TIMES OF MY LIFE. I KNOW I OFTEN FIXATE ON THE NEGATIVITY THAT HAS COME AND GONE OR IS CURRENTLY COMING. ALLOW ME TO BE ABLE TO RECOGNIZE THAT EVERY STORM WILL PASS AND THAT YOU ARE ETERNAL. AMEN.

80

Being Lost

And you were dead in your trespasses and sins in which you previously lived according to the ways of this world, according to the ruler of the power of the air, the spirit now working in the disobedient. We too all previously lived among them in our fleshly desires, carrying out the inclinations of our flesh and thoughts, and we were by nature children under wrath as the others were also.

EPHESIANS 2:1-3

One of the hardest things for many new believers to wrap around their minds is the notion that they were actually lost before knowing Christ. Like many of us that have been lost on a journey, there is a reluctance that comes with knowing you're not where you are supposed to be. Maybe you should have taken a left instead of right. Maybe the directions you were given weren't followed with absolute accuracy. Maybe you've gone south when you probably should have been heading east. Whatever the case may be, we all know that we've been lost, and normally, before we ever realize it, we fight to make sure the way we have chosen is the correct way.

So, when we first became believers, it is not a shock to find that people still have that mentality. Many, in their first steps with Christ, will admit they were lost, but will still carry this notion that their level of being lost was only a little off course, as if they were so close to heaven, but they just should have taken a left instead of a right. They assumed that because they were nice or already somewhat of a good person, or had done good deeds or were kind to others, they would have somehow made it on their own if it weren't for those pesky *little* sins. There is quite the level of arrogance to this kind of thinking.

The reality is that all of us were hopelessly lost before we accepted Christ as our Savior. It doesn't matter which ones of us may have been closer to heaven than the others. Getting to heaven is a lot like traveling to the sun. No matter how close we are to God on this earth, without His grace, we are still hopelessly stranded, moving aimlessly throughout this world looking for heavenly secrets in a very broken world.

In that acknowledgment, we find a humbling truth but discover a tremendous joy. We are humbled because of the fact that the best humanity has to offer is still a broken human. It does not matter how much Scripture we memorize or how many good deeds we may perform; our effort is not what brings us in the presence of our loving Father. It is the very grace of God that removes our lostness, for we have been found. We are no longer lost, and we can see God and His love in our presence and leading our steps each and every day.

LORD, THERE ARE TIMES I LIKE TO PRETEND THAT I HAVE IT ALL TOGETHER. I ASSUME THERE IS SOME CONCEPT OF WORK I CAN DO ON MY END THAT WILL SOMEHOW BRING ME CLOSER TO YOU. LORD, I KNOW IT IS YOUR GRACE, LOVE, AND MERCY THAT ALLOWS ME IN YOUR PRESENCE. BE WITH ME, LORD, AND GUIDE ME EACH AND EVERY DAY. AMEN.

81

Going Mobile!

**Then he said to them, "Go into all the world
and preach the gospel to all creation."**

MARK 16:15

There's a church in a small town in Georgia that does things a little differently than most. The Fourth of July, like in most small towns, is a big deal. Every single organization gets involved in the town festivities. Many of the churches will gather and fly the American flag from their tents so they can show their support of the town festivities. It is also an incredible opportunity for churches to be able to do a little bit of outreach into the community. The problem with each of these is that there is such a sense of uniformity, each church will inevitably blend in with the banks, the mom-and-pop shops, the restaurants, and the chamber of commerce.

Essentially a person has to walk up to one of the tents to find out information about the specific church. They have to go to the tents in order to actually learn anything about the church. This strategy, especially when compared to the identical tents that are lined up, seems a little ineffective for outreach. It's one of the reasons why most of the churches in the small town will go to great lengths to make the inside of their tent spectacular with various games, prizes, gimmicks, and flashy forms of church information. Admittedly, it's eye-catching, but it comes across as shallow.

It's one of the reasons the church mentioned earlier has abandoned the idea of tents for the festival. Instead of renting a space for a tent, they asked the town for the chance to "go mobile." The town didn't exactly understand what they were talking about. I'm sure the mayor assumed they would simply walk around the town square in their church shirts—giving out pamphlets or something of the sort. What they did not plan for was the implementation of carts. Instead of one tent filled with items for the eight ministries going on at their church, they had eight carts for each ministry being pushed around the town square. The tactic was an enormous success.

When the other churches came to the pastor and asked about why he decided to go in the direction of the carts, his answer was relatively simple. He told the other pastors, "Each of us knows the reality of what the Bible has told us to do, and yet, so many of us choose to do the exact opposite. We have been told to 'Go!' We make our churches loftier and fill it with more and more programs in order to get people in, but what are we doing as far as going *out*?"

The next year, there was a new rule against going mobile. If you were going to have an organized presence, you had to have a tent, but still something was different. The tents were still there, but they were no longer filled with church members. Instead, you'd find a couple staff, maybe one or two people in lay-leadership, but outside the tent you'd find the members of the church outside the tent, actually connecting with the community.

LORD, REMIND ME OF THE JOY THAT IS FOUND IN GOING MOBILE. ALLOW ME TO FIND OPPORTUNITIES OUT IN THE WORLD WHERE MY FOCUS IS ON YOU AND BRINGING PEOPLE TO KNOW YOU. AMEN.

82

Good Children

**Sons are indeed a heritage from the LORD,
offspring, a reward. Like arrows in the hand
of a warrior are the sons born in one's youth.
Happy is the man who has filled his quiver with
them. They will never be put to shame when
they speak with their enemies at the city gate.**

PSALM 127:3–5

wo brothers that had now become young men were sitting with their mother and father during the holiday season. As much as they hated to admit it to their parents, they still did not have all of the little nuances of life figured out just yet. They were struggling to pay their bills on time. They were trying to be good husbands, and they were preparing for the upcoming responsibilities of becoming fathers. As they sat their with their wives at the dinner table, one of them finally asked their parents, "Mom, Dad, when did you guys realize you had become successful as adults? I feel like you guys always seemed to have it all together when we were being raised. Do you find out before or after you have kids?"

The two young men began debating over which came first. The younger one claimed that it was an almost automatic response when the child was born, whereas the older one assumed that it was something that was gained during the preparation for the child. The father smirked at his wife as their two sons' debate started to devolve into their usual arguments as children. After a few moments of conversation that had been mixed with little critiques and sarcastic comments, they finally had enough of each other and asked their father which one was correct.

The mother and father looked at each other and whispered into each others' ears as the boys anxiously awaited to find out which one of them was correct. After a few tense moments, the father finally looked at his sons and said, "You don't ever really know if you're a successful adult until you witness the result of the people you've influenced. It doesn't happen when you find out that your wife is pregnant. It doesn't happen when your child is born. It doesn't happen when your child graduates kindergarten, middle school, high school, or college. It doesn't happen when your child has a child. The moment you realize you've been a successful adult, is when you see your children care about others; love their wives; and want to know how to be better men. So . . . I guess you could say I just found out."

Many of us constantly look for that next picture of success. We constantly are trying to figure out what the right steps to take will be. A wise man once said that those that are successful are normally too busy to be looking for it. This is not a plug for busyness, but it points to the notion of realizing that if you are doing what you should be doing, the joy of success will come on its own. You don't have to search for it.

LORD, THANK YOU FOR THE MOMENTS IN MY LIFE THAT HAVE BEEN SUCCESSFUL. I KNOW THERE ARE TIMES I CAN FIXATE ON THE NEXT STEP SO MUCH THAT I FORGET TO BE THANKFUL ABOUT WHAT IS HAPPENING IN THE PRESENT. REMIND ME TO THINK ON WHAT YOU HAVE GIVEN ME TODAY AND ALLOW TOMORROW TO BE JUST THAT, TOMORROW. AMEN.

83

Story Time

So faith comes from what is heard, and what is heard comes through the message about Christ.

ROMANS 10:17

Peter had lived the life of an adventurer. He had traveled the world in the military. He had learned various languages while serving in the mission field. He had seen some of the ancient wonders of the world. He had climbed mountains, swam through the deepest of oceans, jumped off cliffs, and even had a more than a few brushes with death. By the time he was twenty-eight, he had seen just about every corner of the globe. Still, there was nothing quite as wondrous as the moment he met his wife. He settled down, got a job, and had two beautiful girls—now, with a boy on the way. Something his young daughters had come to love was story time.

With structure, Peter would recount his adventures to his daughters. He would spend ten minutes each night telling them of all the pitfalls, successes, and funny mishaps that he had been through during his life. Story time was used as a bartering chip with his young girls in order to get ready for bed. The longer they took to get in bed, the shorter amount of time they would have to listen to their father's stories. It had become a nightly ritual in their household. Eat dinner. Take a bath. Set clothes out for the next day. Brush teeth. Get in bed, and finally, story time. If there was ever a night their father was out of town or unable to give the story for that night, he would even record a little message for his girls—giving a story for them as they drifted to sleep.

There is a certain joy in hearing our Father's story. For those young girls, they are quick to discuss the reality in knowing that their day was just wrong if they had not heard from their father. We should be no different. God has given us His story through His Word. Each and every one of us has access to learning of the all-encompassing story that is the Bible. When we take the time to read God's story and all those who are involved with it, we gain a joy in knowing just a little bit more about Him. When we seek Him out each day through Scripture, our desire and joy in hearing from our Father grows more and more each and every day.

So, pick up His Word. Read through it with joy. It is not simply a book that was written thousands of years ago. It contains the stories of our heavenly Father that recounts all of the events of those who have come to know Him and have made Him known. How can we not have a greater joy than when we are learning more and more about our Father?

FATHER, I ADMIT I AM IN NEED OF SOME STORY TIME. I KNOW I HAVE ALLOWED THE DISTRACTIONS OF THE WORLD TO KEEP ME FROM LEARNING MORE AND MORE ABOUT YOU. PUT IN ME A DESIRE TO LEARN MORE ABOUT YOU AND BRING ME CLOSER TO YOU EACH DAY. AMEN.

84

Challenge Cards

**But as for you, exercise self-control in
everything, endure hardship, do the work
of an evangelist, fulfill your ministry.**

2 TIMOTHY 4:5

In an office building for a Christian corporation, there are challenge cards that have been passed out among the employees. These challenge cards are simple in nature. They have three blank lines on both sides. One side is dedicated to the notion of prayer. The other is to be used for having gospel conversations with individuals that are *unchurched*, a term that has been used en lieu of *lost*. At first, some in the office were a little reluctant to take part in the challenge. They assumed it was a little formulaic. It was already obvious there were people that needed prayer and there were people that needed to know about the gospel. What they did not understand, however, was that the point of the card went much deeper than simply writing down names of people.

After a few months, new cards would be handed out and new names would be written or the same names would be written if they were still in need of either prayer or the hearing of the gospel. Even though there were some that still struggled with the concept there was still the same participation with the writing of the names. After a while, however, something began to change.

New names were written and instead of the regular passing out of cards every few months, there was the desire for more cards. People started requesting stations for the cards so they could pick up more as needed. There was a little bit of joy starting to form over the cards. Finally, after about a year of the cards being used throughout the office building, one of the workers accidentally acknowledged the point of the cards in a discussion over using the cards.

He simply said, "At first, I understood that the cards were to add intentionality to what we do in our daily lives, and that's exactly what they did, but I suppose I did not understand the depth of the point of the cards." For many of us, it takes something simple in order to make a deep impact, and yet, we often overlook that concept because of its simplicity. Yes, writing a name down on a card might initially give a notion of why we're put here, but the daily viewing of those names is what brings the responsibility of knowing those people and their need for Christ.

Because of that, take the challenge. Write three names that need prayer and three names that don't know the gospel. Pray for them. Connect with them, and share time with them. There will be a joy unlike any other in the time that is spent with them.

LORD, ALLOW ME TO TAKE THE CHALLENGE OF INTENTIONALLY THINKING OF THOSE WHO NEED TO HEAR MORE ABOUT YOU. I KNOW THAT SPREADING YOUR NAME IS IMPORTANT, BUT I KNOW EVEN MORE THAT THERE IS JOY IN SHARING YOU WITH PEOPLE. AMEN.

85

Were You Raised in a Barn?

**"Therefore don't worry about tomorrow,
because tomorrow will worry about itself.
Each day has enough trouble of its own."**

MATTHEW 6:34

Christy and Kenneth are both house flippers. They started flipping weeks after their marriage. They have made a little bit of wealth in the short time of flipping. They've even gotten their schedule down to being in and out of a house in about four months, and then, they buy the next one and move into it. The rules are simple. As long as there is at least one livable room in the home and working plumbing, they will buy it, renovate it, and then, sell it. After three years, they have made nearly a million dollars buying, flipping, and selling. Their goal in doing this was to set themselves up in such a way where they can start a family with a good financial foundation. Their plan was to have five years under their belt before they had children, but as they say in the flipping world, "The plan never goes according to plan."

They were working on the renovation of a barn in order to sell as an additional guesthouse on a thirty-acre plot of farmland. As they were wrapping up the project, Christy broke the news to her husband about the new life that was coming into their lives. What was ironic about this was they were working on a project that they had always wanted to end with in their career. They assumed they would find another in the next two years and settle there, but nevertheless, it seemed that the time had come to settle a little earlier than they had anticipated.

As Kenneth placed the final beam in place, he turned to find his wife—holding a onesie that said, "Yes, I was raised in a barn." As tears began to well in his eyes, he held his wife, both excited and nervous about the future. Would they be ready? Had they saved enough money for this moment? Was this the right place? As his mind began to race, his wife took his hand and guided him to the window that he had just installed, out of the window he could see a three-bedroom farmhouse that had yet to be flipped. He saw a rope swing on a large oak tree that would have to be replaced, and looked out at old fields that had not been harvested in years. He saw opportunity, and even though he had not realized it until then, God had placed him at the right place, at the right time. He let go of his wife's hand and wrapped his arm around her shoulder and said, "This will be the nursery."

Many times, we wonder about whether or not things will fall into place the way we expect them to. The fact is, they rarely do; our timing is not God's timing. We can place expectations on our lives all we want, but these expectations only come to fruition if they are within the confines of God's perfect timing. There's a reason we call it perfect timing. It is because of the joy that is found in that timing that is outside of our own understanding.

LORD, I KNOW THERE ARE TIMES I EXPECT THE TIME LINE OF MY LIFE TO FLOW THE WAY I SEE FIT. TAKE AWAY THIS SENSE OF ARROGANCE AND ALLOW ME TO ACCEPT THAT ALL WILL HAPPEN THE WAY YOU WANT IT TO HAPPEN. AMEN.

86

Dirt Drawings

**Before the mountains were born, before
you gave birth to the earth and the world,
from eternity to eternity, you are God.**

PSALM 90:2

There's an artist in Arizona who has become a bit of an internet sensation because of his artwork in the dirt. His canvas is the ground. His medium is the dirt, and as the sun rises and falls throughout the day, the depth of the drawing changes more and more. The drawings started out small, but over time, he started to use entire lots to make a vast array of scenes in one drawing. What's even more interesting is he starts in the center and works his way to the outside, making a picture that has not been corrupted or ruined by the footsteps of the artist. With the desert winds and the potential for the rare rain, these drawings are inevitably temporary.

This inevitability, however, does not stop the artist from gathering his tools, working in the dirt, grabbing a picture, and moving on to the next piece of art. Many critics have often pointed out that his art is something that does not seem to make a great deal of sense because of its temporary nature. After all, why would one go to the trouble of creating something if it is only going to disappear in a matter of hours? The artist's response is one that teaches a great deal about many aspects of our daily lives.

According to him, nothing in this world is permanent. Does that mean that it should not be celebrated? Does it mean that we are not allowed to find joy in the things that are temporary? Why would we ever look at any of these things as anything less than a gift? As a Christian artist, he went a step further. He remarked, "All of the things of this world are temporary, but the joy I have in the Lord is as eternal as He is."

Many things in this world are not necessarily bad, but when we place the role of the eternal on what is temporary, we find false hope. Faith and hope are feelings that are reserved for what is eternal. It does not mean we can't find joy in the temporary. Like the gift of creativity, an artist can find joy in the art that he or she creates. That joy can only grow deeper when we realize who the "Gifter" of those special gifts actually is. When we acknowledge that the joy of our gifts is really from the joy of knowing who gave them, we can only find a deeper joy in all that we accomplish or create, even if it only seems temporary.

LORD, I KNOW I HAVE A TENDENCY TO LOOK AT THE TEMPORARY AS ETERNAL. REMIND ME EACH AND EVERY DAY THAT IT IS YOU WHO IS ETERNAL, AND THERE IS A JOY LIKE NONE OTHER IN RECOGNIZING THAT. AMEN.

87

Scientific Campfire

**"I know that you can do anything and
no plan of yours can be thwarted."**

JOB 42:2

Every year while the cool of spring still reigns over the upcoming summer, a church will have a little camp night for all of the upcoming 6th graders at the church. Before they go into the perils of being seen as a youth in the church, the children's minister plans one more event just to allow the young kids to have a night to just be that, kids. It's a mixture of emotions. The children's minister has known some of these children since they were too young to even walk or speak, and now, she was responsible for handing these kids off to the youth minister, who, in her opinion was a little too "go with the flow." Nevertheless, she had to trust they would be taken care of and placed in good hands.

Something, however, that she decided to change this year was to have her husband, a science teacher, help her with the event. He normally helped from the perspective of a chaperone, but she wanted him to be able to have a more involved role with the kids this year. So, in a way to make the night a little more mysterious, he made a campfire. He did not do this in the traditional sense of rubbing sticks together or lighting a match. Instead, he decided to take the more scientific approach. He decided to mix a couple of chemicals together that upon mixing would ignite and make a small fire.

The kids were amazed. They had never seen such a thing. One of them asked another kid, "How did he do that?" The other responded with Sunday school confidence, "It was Jesus." The husband looked down with a smile— knowing he could have technically just let the child's assumption rest at that, but he decided to go a little deeper. He explained to the children that science is simply the study of how God came to do what God has done. The campfire was made through the use of chemicals heat each other to the point that a flame is produced.

The boys were confused, "So God didn't make the fire?" One of the boys asked. The husband put another mixture on top of the fire, making the blaze change color and grow in size. The children's eyes were lit by the different colors of the fire and in their amazement the husband said, "God has allowed the fire to be. Science simply discovered one of the many ways He allows it."

When we discuss God's sovereignty, we almost get lost in the mystery of all that could mean and forget the joy that comes from the little things in which we find thanksgiving: the air we breathe, the rain that brings life, and yes, the fire that brings light and warmth. God allows for these things to exist so we may understand them scientifically, but their existence is one that is solely dependent on the sovereignty of God.

LORD, I TAKE JOY IN KNOWING IT IS YOU THIS IS IN CONTROL. THERE ARE TIMES THAT I DOUBT. THERE ARE TIMES THAT I FORGET YOU ARE GOD AND I AM NOT. REMIND ME DAILY OF THIS REALITY. AMEN.

88

Big Bad Wolf

God is our refuge and strength, a helper who is always found in times of trouble.

PSALM 46:1

Have you ever heard the story of the three little pigs? There are many variations of the story, but no matter which story you read, there are always three little pigs and a wolf who wants to be let in. Each time the wolf encounters one of the three little pigs, he demands entry, and each time, the three little pigs protest and deny his entry by the powers of their hairs on their chinny-chin-chins. With this denial, the wolf becomes enraged, takes a deep breath, and blows down the houses of the first two pigs.

Now before we start applauding the lung capacity of the wolf, we need to understand the construction of these first two homes has left quite a bit to be desired. The first one is made of hay, which most of us still probably try to wonder the logistics of such a house standing let alone being blown down. The second one is made of sticks, which admittedly is a good home, but any strong gust can blow over stacked twigs no matter the formation they may have been stacked. The third house, however, is the place of refuge. One of the pigs had mastered the art of masonry and constructed a home of brick. The only breath that has been able to topple brick homes are those that are normally accompanied by a hurricane. This big bad wolf is not capable of such a feat.

Believe it or not, the story has often held the fear of many children when they think about the Big Bad Wolf. A few of them even go as far as assuming that if they leave their brick homes, they won't stand a chance against the wolf. Though unintended, this has a very strong Christian message. The overall message of the story points to the importance of family and of having a safe place when trouble comes.

As Christians, we know that any time trouble is on the horizon, we have a refuge and strength that we can turn to. We take joy in knowing that the fears and frustrations of the world pale in comparison to the refuge and safety we find when we are in the presence of our heavenly Father.

When the huffing and puffing of the world attempts to blow down everything we have come to know and love, know there is a God who loves and protects you. That any frustration is one that is temporary for Christ has already conquered the world.

LORD, THANK YOU FOR BEING MY REFUGE WHEN THE WORLD HUFFS AND PUFFS IN MY DIRECTION. I KNOW THERE ARE TIMES I AM AFRAID OF THE BIG BAD WOLVES IN MY LIFE, BUT REMIND ME EACH AND EVERY DAY OF THE LOVE YOU HAVE SHOWN ME, AND THAT IN YOUR REFUGE, I CAN FIND STRENGTH. AMEN.

89

Expense Reports

**Though the fig tree does not bud and there is no
fruit on the vines, though the olive crop fails and
the fields produce no food, though the flocks
disappear from the pen and there are no herds
in the stalls, yet I will celebrate in the LORD;
I will rejoice in the God of my salvation!**

HABAKKUK 3:17–18

In every job, no matter how much joy one may find, there is always something that makes it, well, a job. There are always more than a couple annoyances that sprinkle the workplace each and every day that makes a responsibility look more and more like a burden. For some, it is the tedious piecing together of a spreadsheet once a month. For others, it is the frustration of having a certain duty that they might have been "voluntold" to do. For Taylor, it is the time-taking frustration of having to complete a quarterly expense report. He does his best to keep track of all of the expenses he's created on business trips, but every now and again, an expense pops up that causes him to question its purpose, and that seems to frustrate him even further.

This, of course, is no reason to leave a career. Anyone in the office can tell you that he loves his job. There are just little bumps in the road that frustrate him. For many of us, even if we don't have to deal with expense reports or spreadsheets can probably attest to having similar emotions in our daily lives. We hate all of the little frustrations that come up and keep us from living our lives exactly the way we wish to live them. Does this mean we would forfeit the lives we have as we know them? Of course, not! There is so much joy in our lives that we naturally have a desire to hold onto them. Yes, the joy in working may come at a cost of an exhausted mind, body, and spirit, but this, by no means, communicates that the joy is not worth the work.

Are there going to be difficult seasons in life? Yes. Are there gong to be moments where you want to just throw your hands in the air? Definitely, but the joy is always worth the frustration. Taylor may despise every moment of that expense report, and if that were the only part of his job, none of us would blame him if he decided to walk away from those responsibilities. Taylor, however, will tell you that's not why he does the work he does. He goes to work for the relationships he's built, for the work he has accomplished and gets to take part in, and for the God he loves.

Think about all of the little "expense reports" in your life. Have you allowed your focus to move to them instead of the joy you find in your daily work? Hold onto the joy in knowing that you were placed where you are for a reason, and that even though the road may be difficult now, it is merely a bump. There's plenty of road ahead.

LORD, I KNOW I HAVE BEEN GUILTY OF FOCUSING ON THE BUMPS IN THE ROAD. I KNOW I ALLOW MYSELF TO FIXATE ON THE LITTLE FRUSTRATIONS OF THE WORLD. REMIND ME EACH DAY OF THE JOY THAT COMES IN KNOWING YOU AND THE WORK YOU HAVE GIVEN ME. AMEN.

90

The Ring Box

**"For where your treasure is, there
your heart will be also."**

LUKE 12:34

Something that every woman has come to know is the significance of the ring box. Before they even see the ring inside of it, they are normally overwhelmed with emotion whenever their future husband bends one knee and humbles himself—asking the woman he loves to spend the rest of her life with him. The significance of an engagement is obviously centered around the action of making a proposal to spend one's life with another person you love, but there's still something special about the ring box.

We all know what I'm talking about. Like the shell of a clam, it shuts tightly, creating a little bit of an obstacle when one tries to open it. The opening contains two shallow but soft cushions that are pressed together so closely that they hold the ring in place to the point at which even when the box is turned upside down, the ring will not fall out of its box. The outside of the box, however, is what stands out in every mind. The outside is completely covered in velvet.

Have you ever given any thought as to why that is? Why, of all materials, would velvet be the choice for the covering of the ring box? Well, velvet is one of the more expensive fabrics. Most of the time it is made with some form of cotton, but the most treasured possessions often go in a box covered in velvet that has been made from silk, which can cost several hundred dollars per yard.

For many, the sight of the box alone is almost an exact indicator of the treasure that lies inside, and believe it or not, the treasure is not necessarily the ring. It's the promise that the ring represents. The ring is a physical representation of the promise of a lifelong relationship. The treasure inside may be a diamond, but the joy from the sight of the treasure is not just about the shiny object inside of the box; it is about the promise of a loving commitment that will last during the good times and the bad.

In a way, many of us are like the ring box, carrying with us the eternal promise of God's love. When people see us, do they understand we are carrying an unseen treasure? Do they wonder what's on the inside that brings us so much joy in our daily lives, or do they assume we're just another empty box? Our relationship with Christ is a treasure. Shouldn't our outside show that something precious is living on the inside?

LORD, YOU ARE MY TREASURE. I KNOW THERE ARE TIMES I LIVE LIKE THERE IS NOTHING ON THE INSIDE, BUT I KNOW THERE IS SOMETHING PRECIOUS LIVING IN ME. I KNOW IT IS THE ETERNAL GIFT OF SALVATION THAT YOU HAVE GIVEN THROUGH THE SACRIFICE OF YOUR SON ON THE CROSS. REMIND ME EACH AND EVERY DAY TO ACT LIKE I AM LIVING WITH SOMETHING PRECIOUS. AMEN.

91

" I've Got Extra . . . "

**Don't neglect to do what is good and to share,
for God is pleased with such sacrifices.**

HEBREWS 13:16

In many school districts, there is the implementation of a snack time between breakfast and lunch. It is only fifteen minutes, but it is becoming more and more important, according to child psychologists, for children to get a little break throughout the day in order to refocus and find better productivity throughout the day. Students will gather in the back of the room to get a little snack from their backpacks that their parents have sent with them. Some parents send a little pastry, or some fruit, or vegetables, or even a heavy appetizer from their favorite restaurant. The students have come to love it, and the parents generally go to great lengths to ensure that their child has a snack during this little break in the day. Nevertheless, there is always at least one child that does not move from his or her desk during the time to go and get a snack that has been packed for them.

They normally use the time to go to the restroom, grab a sip of water, or even just go on a short walk in the halls. One student in particular had shown this behavior to the point at which he had almost developed a rhythm. As soon as the teacher would announce that snack time had started, he would ask to go to the restroom and buy a snack from the snack machine. Because he was such a good student, the teacher always respected his request to leave the room and return for snack time. The boy, however, never returned with a snack.

He would always claim that he ate it on the way back to the room, but a quick look at the cameras would prove that all the boy was doing was going to the restroom, getting a sip of water, and returning to the outside of the classroom and sitting next to the door for a couple of minutes before opening the door. The poor boy was never getting a snack.

So, the teacher, in all her kindness, started packing a few extra carrot sticks with her during snack time. She would eat a few and then when the boy returned, she would go to him and say, "I've got extra . . ." The boy would act, for a moment, as if he did not need it, but would always accept it, and then months later, he would come to her with an extra couple of apple slices and said, "I've got extra . . ."

For many of us, we forget just how far a small gesture of generosity can go. Generosity is an interesting activity. On one hand, it shows love by giving something to someone else. On the other, it brings joy to both parties when they know the level of care that has gone into loving someone. Generosity does not always take a grand gesture. Sometimes, the greatest joy can be found by giving out just a little extra.

FATHER, YOU HAVE GIVEN ME SO MUCH. REMIND ME TO SHOW GENEROSITY EACH DAY WITH THE THINGS YOU HAVE GIVEN ME. PUT PEOPLE IN MY LIFE THAT NEED MY GENEROSITY AND REMIND ME TO LIVE A LIFE OF GIVING A LITTLE EXTRA EACH AND EVERY DAY. AMEN.

92

Returning to Rent

**When arrogance comes, disgrace follows,
but with humility comes wisdom.**

PROVERBS 11:2

There is never a harsher feeling than having to sell a home and return to the renting world, and yet, we hear about more and more individuals renting out apartments in order to save a few dollars, eliminate debt, or take a season to build a home to their liking. For some, it is an optional decision. For others, there is no other option. Whatever the case may be, there are two things that flourish from such decision-making: trust and humility.

Many young couples are downsizing to make sure their needs are met for their future. They don't want to have to live under the thumb of debt. As much as they hate to admit it, getting out from under that thumb sometimes requires them to move in with parents, or rent out a basement, or move into an apartment. Whatever the case may be, it is always a difficult decision to make.

This reality paints a bigger picture in our daily lives. As much as we may hate to admit it, there is something that is a little disheartening about the notion of taking a step back. We hate the idea of it to be completely honest. When we take a step back, it feels like we've made a mistake or we've made a decision that turned out to be an utter failure. It is never easy for us to make that kind of decision. It is never easy for us to admit when we need to regroup.

The reality is, however, that there can be a great deal of joy in taking a moment to return to a better footing. It may seem difficult to return to it. Think about how much work you did just to get where you are, but this is not the attitude of humility. When we think about all of the work we've accomplished in order to get our current footing—when we have this mind-set, we can fall prey to our own pride. We can look at the past and lose our thankfulness for having the steps that have led us to our current position.

The fact is that life is going to have ups and downs. When we cement ourselves in a place that seems unstable, we will inevitably fall. It's one of the many reasons why we point to the notion that there is never a fall quite like the one that comes from a prideful spirit. Take joy in humility. It may not be fun to take a step down. It may feel like taking a step down is the wrong move, but sometimes, it takes a step down to reset before you can step back up the right way. There is nothing wrong with that. In fact, taking a step in humility is one that always ends in joy.

LORD, I KNOW I DON'T WANT TO TAKE THE STEPS THAT FEEL LIKE MISHAPS. HUMILITY IS NOT ALWAYS AN EASY CHOICE. REMIND ME THAT JOY IS ON THE OTHER SIDE OF A JOY THAT'S MADE IN HUMILITY. ALLOW ME TO DISCOVER THE JOY IN DOING WHAT IS RIGHT EVEN WHEN IT INITIALLY FEELS LIKE AN INCONVENIENCE.

93

Prep Time

**A horse is prepared for the day of battle,
but victory comes from the LORD.**

PROVERBS 21:31

Ask any introvert and they will be quick to tell you they absolutely detest the notion of getting ready for a meeting, especially when it is one in which they have to present. Their heart beats just a little bit faster. Their hands will typically shake with a little uneasiness, and they won't exactly know how to feel when all of it is over. Typically, they will go off on their own in a way to recharge from the mental exhaustion of having to discuss business information to a crowd of people. In order to overcome this mental anguish, many introverts will prepare for hours on top of hours to the point at which they've already guessed what kinds of questions will be thrown at them during their presentation. Because of this preparation, a great many of them will assume the worst if they have not had ample time to prepare for certain presentations.

As difficult as it is for us to admit, all of us have a tinge of introverted behavior in our own psyche. All of us have something that makes us so nervous that we feel the need to prepare for it as its approach becomes a reality. This prepping is something that is useful, but more often than not, this focus can often turn into a form of idolatry. Think about it for a moment. Regardless of whether or not they are an introvert is not the point. We all know someone that puts so much focus on their preparation that when they feel they have not prepared themselves to the degree that they assume, they place an automatic assumption they will fail. This emotion is not from a lack of preparation. It is from a place of worry—an emotion where joy has no opportunity to flourish and grow.

Don't get me wrong. Preparation is a good thing. It is something in which the wisest among us will recognize its worth, but putting such a focus on preparation is a notion that will always lead to worry. When our focus is put solely on the plan and not what we've been called to do, the moment that the plan immediately falls apart, we take on the emotion of assuming that the sky is falling and the world is over.

Preparation is key in everything we care about. To prepare for something is to show how much you care about that thing, but when push comes to shove, there are going to be things that go wrong. There are going to be moments when something doesn't go according to plan. Something will always pop up where someone was not prepared, and that's okay. Recognizing that you've done your best. You've made a plan and stick to it. If something goes wrong, choose joy over anxiety.

LORD, I ADMIT THERE ARE TIMES I HAVE BECOME SO FOCUSED ON DOING WELL I'VE FORGOTTEN HOW IMPORTANT IT IS TO RELAX WHEN SOMETHING DOESN'T GO ACCORDING TO PLAN. REMIND ME EACH DAY THAT I AM NOT THE ONE WHO HAS TO BE PERFECT, AND WHEN SOMETHING GOES WRONG, EVERYTHING WILL STILL WORK OUT AS IT SHOULD. AMEN.

94

Have a Little Faith

**"For I know the plans I have for you"—this is the
LORD's declaration—"plans for your well-being,
not for disaster, to give you a future and a hope."**

JEREMIAH 29:11

Donnie is someone who only makes a decision if he knows all of the possible outcomes. He does not like to leap before looking. This is not to say he doesn't have a touch of impulsivity. Whenever something catches his interest, he is quick to act, but before he makes a move, he makes plans, does research, asks friends if they've done the activity he's interested in, and then, finally will make a move toward taking part in this planned adventure.

If there is anything that Donnie hates, however, it is the notion of going with the flow. He is not one to just get in the car with friends and "just go somewhere." It is a notion that he, in fact, has come to despise. So much so that people know not to invite him unless there is a plan already on the table. This seems like a pretty unpleasant life. Does it not?

If we were truly honest with ourselves, though, many of us have a touch of this kind of behavior. We want to know what's happening next. We want to be able to have some sort of understanding in the midst of all the chaos. The problem is, however, sometimes there's a point to the chaos. Maybe we are supposed to learn or notice something in the unpredictable moments of life.

The fact is, there might be a little bit of joy that's been hidden in the moments that are outside of your understanding.

When we talk about going with the flow, we are not talking about living a carefree life. We are talking about trust. Just because you can't see the path's end does not mean you should not be on the path. Just because you may not know the next move does not meant you should not take part in all that is happening around you. Trust God. Know that He is in control, and for goodness sake, do us all a favor, and have a little faith.

HEAVENLY FATHER, I KNOW I DO MY BEST TO
KNOW EVERY PART OF THE JOURNEY IN SO MANY
THINGS. REMIND ME TO HAVE FAITH IN THE
MOMENTS WHEN I CANNOT SEE WHAT IS COMING
NEXT. ALLOW ME TO TAKE MORE CHANCES AND
OPPORTUNITIES, AND TRUST THAT THE PATH YOU
HAVE CALLED ME TO WILL END IN JOY. AMEN.

95

The Coloring Book

**"But even the hairs of your head have all
been counted. So don't be afraid; you are
worth more than many sparrows."**

MATTHEW 10:30–31

Little Reese loves a good coloring book. The more intricate the drawing, the greater joy she finds in filling the blank spots with color. She enjoys fantastical scenes that are filled with castles, warriors, and mythical creatures, but she will show just as much joy over coloring a page that depicts the Amazon jungles. There's something about the way the pictures just seem like half of the beauty that makes Reese grow in excitement over the prospect of making it pop with color.

Even when she finds a page that could only use one or two colors, like a tree, she goes to the trouble of coloring each leaf with just a slightly different shade of green to make the color pop in a way that evolves her box of crayons to being childlike to that of artwork. In fact, she would even argue that she enjoys that kind of coloring even more. According to her, there's something special about coloring leaves. From a distance, if you were to simply look at a tree and discern what color the leaves were showing, you would, obviously, say, "Green," but upon further inspection, it becomes fairly noticeable that there is the slightest variation between the leaves. Simply put, even when two things in this world appear to be identical, there is something about them that makes them different.

What a joyful concept! For so many of us, we often struggle with the notion that there is nothing special about us. There is nothing that sets us apart from the rest of the world. This could not be farther from the truth. Even identical twins can notice their differences. Why should we be no different? The fact of the matter is that God made each and every one of us uniquely. There is no one else on this planet who is *exactly* like us. In that we can take a special amount of joy. Even in the days when we feel like there is nothing of note about us, we can know out of the billions of people that have ever existed, God never made anyone that was just like you.

LORD, I ADMIT THERE ARE DAYS WHEN I FEEL LIKE THERE IS NOTHING SPECIAL ABOUT ME. I KNOW I SOMETIMES FEEL AS IF I AM JUST ANOTHER LEAF ON A TREE. REMIND ME EACH DAY THAT YOU HAVE MADE ME UNIQUELY, AND IN THAT UNIQUE MAKING, THERE IS A UNIQUE LOVE. AMEN.

96

Giggle Fits

**"In my Father's house are many rooms; if not,
I would have told you. I am going away to
prepare a place for you. If I go away and prepare
a place for you, I will come again and take you
to myself, so that where I am you may be also.
You know the way to where I am going."**

JOHN 14:2–4

Laughter has never been seen as a poor choice of activity. It has, however, had more than one occasion of being poorly timed. We all know what I'm talking about. Everyone enjoys a good laugh, but there is such a thing as a bad timing for that laugh. Most of us can probably remember a time when we've had a finger pointed in our direction for snickering during a sermon, or we've received a scolding for chuckling during a wedding, but there is never a wrath quite like the anger received for catching the giggle fits during a funeral.

For one family, however, it happened during their own father's funeral. This is not to say they weren't grieving. The siblings had already lost their mother, so this was their last parent. This should have been a somber occasion for all of them, and honestly, it started out that way. Family friends and extended family member offered condolences and warm embraces. A slideshow with pictures of their father played over and over. They saw pictures of him at work in the office—wearing a suit and a trademark smirk. They saw him

193

at church, serving the congregation as an elder. The sibling even caught a few pictures of themselves with their father.

One picture, however, stood out. They looked up to find a picture of themselves—smiling with an obviously frustrated father. The picture had been taken moments before the children would be grounded for some past mischievousness. Those that knew the siblings well knew what was coming. The youngest smirked and looked at the oldest while the middle one did her best to keep from laughing, but with every convulsion she tried to repress came a snicker, a snort, and, inevitably, and laugh so contagious that the rest of the sanctuary decided to join.

After the funeral, the pastor asked what caused the laughter. The middle sibling gave a response that I feel so many of us forget at funerals. She said, "Dad's in paradise, and as much as I miss him, I know he is standing before the Father. With that being said, laughing at a picture that brought back a funny memory seems a better choice than to cry over something that should actually be celebrated."

LORD, I KNOW THERE ARE MOMENTS WHERE I INSTINCTIVELY CHOOSE DESPAIR WHEN I SHOULD BE CHOOSING JOY. REMIND ME THAT JOY IS A CHOICE AND THAT THE DWELLING ON PAIN IS SOMETHING THAT HINDERS ME FROM KNOWING A DEEPER JOY IN YOU. AMEN.

97

A Joyful Influence

God replied to Moses, "I AM WHO I AM. This is what you are to say to the Israelites: I AM has sent me to you."

EXODUS 3:14

There's a new profession that has started in the midst of the social media age. Today, we no longer hear the aspirations of fame that revolve around acting, singing, or playing a professional sport. Now, people are evolving in their understanding of fame. They are moving away from the notion of being in front of a $20,000 camera, and instead are realizing they can achieve just as much fame from the camera that has been built into their phones. The aspiration of social media influencing is something that has grown to the point that we are finding more and more people leaving the places that foster fame to realizing any place can be that place depending on the level of lighting the influencer may have access.

These individuals will spend hours and hours creating the perfect video that is short enough to hold the attention of the viewer but has just enough content to shape the viewer into continuing to want a relationship with the videos that have been made. Between subscriptions, follows, double-taps, and likes, there is an almost infinite amount of content that is thrown at us each and every day in hopes it will influence us to constantly return for more.

All of the joy that is gained from this content, however, comes across as shallow in the long run. Sure, we may get a few chuckles or our heart strings pulled during the viewing of the content, but over time, our eyes dull and we end up having an attitude that grows tired of seeing another one of *those* videos.

Something that has never had this kind of attitude in response to it is found in the reading of Scripture. When we leave the attitude of reading it as just another book and realize it is the very Word of God, we are able to move to a level of appreciation over the fact that it is the lasting message of God which has outlived men, cities, and entire civilizations. How can we not respond in joy over the notion of reading a letter from the Creator of the universe? We have access to the history of our people, to the poetry describing the love of God, and to the parables taught by His Son—holding lessons that are still applied to this day. Take joy in knowing that even though we live in a world of influencers vying for our attention, we worship a God who instead of influencing through His actions, He has chosen to simply leave us a book with one message. That message is simple but powerful. God simply tells us, "I am."

DEAR LORD, I KNOW THERE ARE SO MANY PEOPLE THAT ARE FIGHTING FOR MY ATTENTION. I ADMIT THEY DON'T ALWAYS HAVE TO FIGHT HARD. LORD, REMIND ME EACH DAY WHO YOU ARE. THROUGH YOUR WORD, ALLOW ME TO CONSTANTLY FIND JOY IN THE FACT THAT YOU ARE GOD. AMEN.

98

Make a List

And the world with its lust is passing away, but the one who does the will of God remains forever.

1 JOHN 2:17

When Jacob married his wife, he learned very quickly the meaning of the old phrase: "You marry the family." This is not necessarily a bad thing. He loved his in-laws more than most people love theirs, but still, it's always a little jarring to add on another set of holidays to the ones you already celebrate with your own family. Two Christmas meals became four, which was great because there were presents at each gathering. The Fourth of July was now alternated between families, which of course, he liked because there would be a change of scenery for fireworks, and Thanksgiving lunch was ended at two in the afternoon, just in time for Jacob to get in the car and drive two hours to have Thanksgiving dinner. Jacob is still trying to find some level of enjoyment during that holiday, but his wife reminds him that it's acceptable for him to not eat at both.

With the addition of these new holidays, Jacob also gains the opportunity to add wisdom to his collection by striking up conversations with the other men in his newfound family. One of which is his wife's uncle. The man has found great amounts of success over the years. He grew up in a small town, moved to a big city, and worked his way up in a company that supports other businesses across the nation. He's currently two promotions away from leading the corporation, because of his success. Jacob has become obsessed with his uncle-in-law and looks to follow in the man's footsteps. Through the asking of little trade secrets on how to manage one's money and make more of it, Jacob has spoken to the man in a bush-beating fashion frequently. Finally, after a couple of years of knowing the man, he finally asked, "How'd you do it?"

The uncle grinned and gave him a little tidbit of advice. He told him to make a list, fill it with the things he wants in this life and return it to him later in the evening. Jacob excused himself for thirty minutes and then returned with a list—filled with every fanciful material he could imagine. His wife's uncle was sitting next to a fire pit, alone, watching the flames and feeling the heat replace the crisp fall air. Jacob sat next to him and showed him the list, and before he could open his mouth to explain why certain things made the list, the uncle looked it over and tossed it in the fire.

Frustrated, Jacob demanded to know why he threw it in the fire. His uncle said, "I only looked for God. Unless a relationship with God was on the list then it doesn't matter if you spent thirty days on that list. You'll never find joy unless God is first on your list."

Most forget the level of joy that comes from a living relationship with Christ. We assume it's the new car or the big house that's going to be the sustainer for joy. Instead of seeking joy in the next shiny new thing, turn to God and discover a joy that is everlasting.

LORD, I KNOW THERE ARE TIMES WHERE I HAVE FOCUSED ON THE WRONG THINGS TO FULFILL MY NEED FOR JOY. I WANT ALL OF THE NICE THINGS. I WANT TO HAVE THE NEW CAR AND THE BIG HOUSE, AND WHILE THESE AREN'T BAD, REMIND ME EACH DAY THAT IT IS YOU THAT BRINGS TRUE JOY IN THIS LIFE. AMEN.

The "D" Group

They devoted themselves to the apostles' teaching, to the fellowship, to the breaking of bread, and to prayer.

ACTS 2:42

Churches all over the nation have made a move from the large corporate worship to having smaller, intimate sessions with a small group of people. This does not mean that the churches are shrinking or the doors are closing. There is simply an intentional move to bring people closer to God in smaller settings. The large corporate worship is still, very much, happening, but churches are now encouraging individuals to find a group of believers to grow in their understanding of the Bible. Some are called community groups, focus studies, life groups, or even small churches.

A few churches, however, are growing even deeper in this notion of intimate biblical study. Most of the time a small group at church will consist of ten to fifteen members reading the Bible or Bible study and discussing what they've read. These are the kinds of groups where most regularly attending churchgoers are aware of. Some churches have chosen to move forward with "D" groups. The "D" stands for discipleship.

Where most community groups can gloss over a study to have conversation about the application of the study in their lives, a discipleship group takes a slow and deep look at Scripture to gain a better understanding. One group, for instance, studied the book of James in their discipleship group. Three men gathered every Saturday morning before the day truly started and took time to memorize a little bit more of James and discuss the theological implications of the book, one verse at a time. What was the result? Well from this group, the men memorized the entire first chapter and discussed the book as a whole for a few months. After they had completed their discussion on James, they made a difficult, but necessary decision. They separated to form their own groups— studying a new section of the Bible with new faces.

In that, we find the true method of discipleship. Many Christians believe that simply by reciting a prayer through the act of conversion, they've done enough. That is just one very small drop in a very large bucket. We are called to go way deeper than conversion. Conversion without discipleship is like tossing the keys to a new car to a five-year-old and saying, "Good luck!" And yet, so many Christians have walked away from that situation and thought to themselves, "Job well done."

The true joy of knowing Jesus comes through intense study of the Bible with fellow believers. Accepting Christ as our Savior is like swiping dirt away from a treasure chest, revealing the face of the chest. True joy in knowing our Savior comes from the intense process of digging out that very treasure, and that only comes through discipleship.

LORD, I KNOW YOU SENT YOUR SON TO DIE ON THE CROSS FOR ME. ALLOW ME TO BE ABLE TO KNOW YOU MORE EACH AND EVERY DAY THROUGH THE READING AND STUDY OF YOUR WORD. PLACE PEOPLE IN MY LIFE THAT WILL DISCIPLE ME, AND ALLOW ME TO DIG DEEPER IN YOUR WORD THAT CARRIES THE ULTIMATE MESSAGE OF LOVE AND JOY. AMEN.

The Last One

**"But many who are first will be
last, and the last first."**

MATTHEW 19:30

More often than not, to call anything "last" is normally not an enjoyable experience. For those of us who are a little competitive, being last is, well, the last thing we would ever want. We don't want to be picked last or find ourselves last in line. Instead, we want to know how to be first. We want to be the first to discover something, whether it be through knowledge or physical ownership. Being the last one in anything is a notion that many of us would rather not entertain, but what if we choose to be last?

To be placed last is something that none of us would enjoy, but to choose to be last might have a different connotation to it. Obviously we see it on a smaller scale and know exactly what I'm describing. We know what it means to open the door for others, to let someone go ahead of us in line, or to even give up the last of an item to someone who is more in need of it, but what if we went a step further? What if we fought to be last?

I know this sounds like a rather laughable notion, but what if we held the door for people to enter a building we'd have no intention of entering? We were simply there to open the door. What if we purposefully sought out items that individuals need only to give them up instead of taking them for ourselves?

What if the line we were already standing in the back of grew just a little bit longer because we constantly take a step back to let others in front of us. Surely this kind of behavior would look like lunacy, and yet, if you use your imagination, do we see any of these people frowning?

Do we see any of these people scrunching their face as they constantly allow people to go ahead of them? No matter how difficult you may try, it seems even more idiotic to picture someone that shows sacrificial kindness with anything more than joy on their face. When we are forced to be last, it is, at its smallest, an inconvenience, but when we *choose* to be the last one, there is a joy that cannot be explained.

As much as we want this devotion to make you feel joy, we want even more to remind you that true joy comes from living a life that is dedicated to loving Christ and serving others—showing the depth of His love for each and every one of us. When the chances come to allow others to go ahead of you, take it. It's a small taste of joy, but when the opportunity arises to put yourself last, don't shy away from it because even though it may be inconvenient, deep kindness, like joy, is contagious.

DEAR LORD, I KNOW THIS WORLD HAS SUCH A NEED FOR REAL KINDNESS. ALLOW ME TO BE ABLE TO SERVE THOSE AROUND ME WITHOUT A DESIRE FOR ANYTHING IN RETURN. REMIND ME THAT YOU SERVED ME WITH A GIFT THAT COULD NEVER BE PAID BACK AND THAT PRICE WOULD NEVER BE EXPECTED TO BE PAID. AMEN.